My Journey to Faith

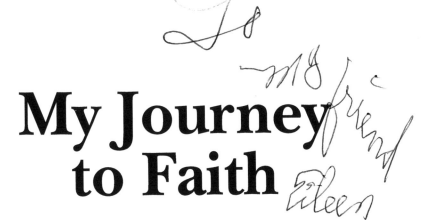

My Journey to Faith

A Memoir

Florence Frazier

BRATHWAITE PUBLISHING
www.brathwaitepublishing.com

Books by Arlene Brathwaite are published by

Brathwaite Publishing
P.O. Box 1202
Albany, New York 12201

Copyright © 2015 by Arlene Brathwaite

ISBN 13: 9780692478882
ISBN: 0692478884

This book was printed in the United States of America.

ACKNOWLEDGMENTS

M any thanks to Mary Dev. Jackson who spent hours deciphering my tremu- lous handwriting from start to finish and to Judy for jump-starting me on the autobiography road.

INTRODUCTION

Jesus loves the little children
All the children of the world
Red and yellow, black and white
They are precious in his sight
Jesus loves the little children of the world.

My Bethel AME Sunday school favorite hymn

Florence Elaine Jackson 1926

It's the songs you sing and the
smiles you wear that make
the sunshine everywhere.
—Anonymous

CHAPTER 1

START OF MY JOURNEY

I was born on August 23, 1923, the third child of James and Clara Johnson-Jackson.

James Jackson (R)

At the time, my sister Helen was three and a half, and my brother Jimmy was two years old, and the family was in the process of moving from Grandma Jackson's to a rental home of our own in Huntington Station, Long Island.

Clara Johnson-Jackson

My earliest memory is of my father carrying me downstairs, with me having a huge patch over my eye. I later learned that I had a serious case of the measles, and the eye was scarred. I sobbed uncontrollably as my mother undressed me for bed at her sister's home. I guess I couldn't deal with her leaving me there just to go with Daddy to the masonic affair. I survived and later found out that my father was one of the founders of the Hunter Squires, Jackson Post number 1218 American Legion at Amityville.

I have no memory of my brother, Jimmy, who died of pneumonia at the age of three. However, just after I turned four, Grandma Jackson came to deliver my brother Howard on October 4, 1927. I remember asking her questions while she washed clothes. I couldn't understand why she wore long black dresses all the time. Years later, my mother declined to answer any questions about them, although I did investigate and find out on my own.

I started kindergarten in September 1928 and felt joy and comfort that overcame my sense of being brushed aside by my sister. I was truly in a world of music, books, and people. By the second week of school, I learned that I was not alone in feeling unwanted. Naomi joined me at the top of the hill. Her sister and mine were quite a few yards ahead of us, commiserating their ill fortune to have "those two tagging along." We have remained friends and asked the sisters for forgiveness for "intruding" in their lives.

Sunday afternoons, I learned more about my family from the Johnson sisters and children since our house was "huge," with a wraparound porch and a backyard with pear and plum trees, berry bushes, a vegetable garden, a barn for our Ford car, and a chicken coop. Several sisters and a sister-in-law gathered to bring each other up-to-date on what was happening in everyone's lives—theirs and their neighbors', employers', brothers', missing sisters', and the numerous "You Know Whos'"—and why the Jacksons didn't move from South Huntington away from "You Know Who."

Our Backyard

The juiciest morsels were the cakes and cookies Clara always had for the children outside. Helen, however, refused to be with "those kids." Since Dad wouldn't take her to the ball game with him, she stayed upstairs and read. I think she heard quite a bit of gossip that she passed on to our cousin Ella, who also refused to come with her mother—although she was indeed somewhat older than Helen.

Helen

Both my grandfathers died in 1923, leaving behind the Jackson wife and family in Massachusetts and Long Island and the Johnson wife and fourteen children in Huntington. Such a large number of males and females interacting with each other—at times as siblings, then adversaries, and then friends—but over the years as my family's support.

This Huntington, Long Island, where I grew up wandered, worked, and was educated in (as my mother before me) was the center (from north to south) of a fish-shaped land mass off the coast of Connecticut and Massachusetts.

Florence Elaine Jackson

Our relatives lived "down the neck" or Hale site, up from the village, in the Station, South Huntington, and then in Amityville. Those walking visits to relatives, church, and school were a normal part of my life.

Happiness is not a state to
arrive at, but a manner
of traveling.
—Margaret Lee Runbeck

CHAPTER 2

GROWING UP

In the summer of 1930, Helen continued her knitting, and I attempted to crochet while keeping an eye on my baby brothers, Howard and George. This year, there was no "watching for Daddy" to round the corner from New York Avenue, swinging his lunch box and waving good-bye to his cousins Frank and Wilfred, who were coming from work on the Long Island Railroad. The Great Depression had begun. Our Thanksgiving and Christmas were somber. Dad got upset when church members and masonics brought food and toys to the house for us. It made him feel "less than a man." At those times, my mother encouraged us to hug Daddy and tell him that we loved him as he sat sobbing in his Morris chair.

George and Howard Jackson

By February 1931, even the bankers and stockbrokers were hit. Many of them took flight from their luxurious skyscraper offices and penthouses.

My Jackson cousins Laura and Alviha Edwards, who were older than Helen and I, were allowed to come visit. We had great jump-rope contests, along with my next-door friends Vera and Naomi. One Saturday in mid-February, the weather permitted great outdoor activities. After several attempts on my turn to jump, the pain in my side was excruciating. I yelled for my mom, and the next thing I knew, I was in the hospital with a ruptured appendix, which kept me there for three months. I shared a room with a schoolmate. We had many food fights (usually peas or beans). We were punished by getting no dessert.

Flo, Naomi, Laura

My father's cousins kept him from self-destructing, and a new baby brother, Norman, was born on March 11, 1930.

The VA hospital at Northport became home for my father, who suffered from the aftermath of poison gas in no-man's-land in World War I in the Argonne Forest of France and the final blow—the loss of job and his inability to provide for his family. Eighteen years later, I saw him at a predischarge home visit to his sister and my cousins in South Huntington.

The days at home following my return from the hospital were filled with new experiences, activities, and others constantly coming and going while I was told by many to do my chores around the house. Some of the activities I wanted to do, like playing outside, but others I didn't like—making sure the boys didn't run in the street; washing Howard's back on Saturday night; walking to Wydanch before sunrise with Aunt Net and cousin Bob to pick huckleberries (blueberries); going with mom to the home-relief store for broken rice, cheese, powdered milk, and flour while Helen stayed home and watched the boys, knowing that our neighbors were available if she needed them. I felt grown up but still missed time with my paper dolls and the freedom of being with Vera and Gloria, my next-door girlfriends.

The family and community rallied around us as when we lost baby brother Norman to pneumonia. One uncle, Roy, paid mom to launder and iron his shirts with "just the right amount of starch in the collar;" another uncle, Van, dropped by "just in case there's anything to do;" and another uncle, Ted, roomed in the nice warm attic and took care of the furnace and plumbing and showed Mom how to repair any electrical appliance, including ironing cords. Aunt Evie came by every other night to bring leftover food from her employer's family and from church affairs. She also encouraged our attendance at Sunday school by promising a taste of pie on our way home. Other churchwomen regularly came by to offer prayer and support.

The new AME minister's tennis playing, NYC-sophisticated son needed a place to stay, and the minister suggested that Mom had the room and could use the cash. So our home was rearranged to accommodate. Coincidently, Isabel, his fiancée, was a nurse in need of someone to launder, starch, and iron her uniforms, so mom's business began.

By the time school was out in June 1932, I understood that although I liked all the people around me, I had stronger feelings for those who were attentive toward me—Mom, Aunt Evie, and Aunt Net. I knew that boys were different physically but also that some were rough, while others, like Mom's brothers, would always be there for me. Helen still distanced herself, although we were expected to "act like sisters" as we walked to AME Sunday school, YMCA Girl Reserves meetings, and school.

In the summer of '32, I was drawing my house in the dusty backyard, paying particular attention to windows, curtains, and where furniture should be, when it was suddenly all destroyed. Howard, George, and their friend Bossi roared through and headed for the neighbor's land as they played cowboys with human hands as guns chasing the illusive Indians with flints. I was devastated and complained loudly to Mom. As a result, she had the chicken coop cleaned out and gave it to me as my house. I made orange crates into furniture and scraps of old clothes into curtains, and whoever visited shared mayonnaise, lettuce, and tomato sandwiches with me.

This same year, my cousin Ella walked with me to the Huntington Station Library since I was not allowed to travel alone away from Church Street. I loved getting books and giving the teacher a written report in September. As a result, I was skipped a semester, but I lost track of my friends along the way.

The winter of 1932–33 was not only snowy but also bitterly cold. Our pipes froze, and Mother directed me to take the path from our backyard to the next street over to Mr. Wagner, the plumber. I dressed in my father's fishing boots, two pairs of mittens, two sweaters under my coat, and hat. My scarf, worn over my head, covered my nose and went around my neck. I stumbled through the snow-covered bramble bushes to reach School Street. This was also was the winter I saw Walter Johnson rolling in the snow at ten years old—his first experience in this white, fluffy stuff, having been born in Georgia. His entire family had just moved into Huntington.

Roller skates were my opportunity to roam the neighborhood and get to know everybody. Home was at number eight Church Street, changed from "First Street," which made sense to us since the lower part of the building next door to us had once housed a dance hall and a factory, and, most recently, was rented as a church. Across the street was a synagogue. In addition to upgrading this multiethnic area called Huntington Station, sidewalks were installed throughout the "Station Neighborhood," so I got to know and talk with the Russian-Jewish Schwartz family, owners of the gas station; the German-Jewish family who had the lumberyard across from our house; the Southern-Italian family next door to us; my classmate from Northern Italy; the Schlesingers (my friend from the hospital); and the Haymers, directly off the Shinnicock Reservation intermarrying with others tribes. There was a Quaker family and, gradually, many other southerners and West Indian families. Huntington Station had its own business district on New York Avenue from Academy Street South to Jericho Turnpike—therefore the village remained somewhat pure Anglo-Saxon.

I grew and learned so much during this time. Oh, no Santa Claus? Each day was an education in school and at home. We visited Nana Johnson in the village after a "decoration day" parade (today known as Memorial Day). This parade had special meaning for her as her father, Moses Smith, died in the Civil War, and the family wasn't awarded his pension until 1891. I watched the tiny woman direct her daughters, Clara and Janet, to get large branches and poke the snake away from the door after the parade at her house. "Send him back up the hill to Indian Joe where he belongs."

We enjoyed visiting Nana and would resist "It's time to go home" until Mom reminded us that staying meant using the outhouse and pumping water. The attraction was that cousin Bob had every toy and sport equipment imaginable. As the only child of Aunt Net and Uncle Dan, they lived with and took care of Nana. But nothing lasts forever. When the youngest Johnson son married and wanted to claim the property before Nana died, the result was that she came to live with us, and then she died within several months. She called me Clara sometimes when I attended her.

Funeral and wakes were held in the home at that time. For Nana's, all the relatives packed into the kitchen, dining room, back porch, front parlor, wraparound porch, front and backyards, plus, standing room only in the garage and chicken coop. Since Nana had not attended the church, the oldest daughter, Fanny, who was a founder and pillar of the Bethel AME Church and married to Reverend Lonzo, was brought in to officiate. I didn't remember what was said by whom. I do remember watching a bed bug crawl up Ben Hendrickson's jacket, waiting for it to reach his neck and bite him, and watching to see whether he would brush it off or squash him.

Uncle Ted had "no-work days" during the winter as he only had to attend the cows at milking time. Otherwise, he did chores for Mom and taught various card games to us after school. I understood basic algebra from playing pinochle. I learned and developed a "poker face" whenever necessary.

Summer came soon enough. In 1934, we planned a Labor Day weekend motor trip to New Jersey, where Uncle Roy and Aunt Maym lived. I was in pain with cramps and was diaper wrapped, on my way to womanhood. I was miserable but consoled by pistachio ice cream. I would have to look forward to this every month? No wonder Helen was so angry sometimes. This shared misery was the beginning of our positive sister relationship. I noticed the books she read and listened to "Lady Day," and other musicians on the Victrola, which she commanded. I continued clipping poems from the *Saturday Evening Post* that someone dropped by the house and filling my scrapbook.

What a difference in the attitude at school too. We girls were assigned to homemaking classes every day while the boys were assigned to shop. In addition to our civics, geography, English, and gym classes, we could also sign up for chorus or orchestra. I loved every minute at school and at home when Mom put more expectations on us in terms of who taught what and when and where the next outing was. We had been to the *Daily News* office in New York City to get an understanding of publishing and on a trip to the shipyard where we toured an ocean liner from top to bottom and bow to stern. Museums and libraries were a must.

By the age of thirteen, I had made my first pineapple upside-down cake, biscuits, and berry shortcake. I designed and modeled my first two-piece dress at a community school affair. I was hooked on clothes design.

There just weren't enough hours in a day anymore. Saturdays were cleanup days—our part of the room and checking to see that "the boys" did the same— and then off to the YMCA Girl Reserves meeting while the boys went to the movies where they were able to see the same western show over and over until I got them out to go home for dinner. My piano lessons were early Saturday mornings or immediately after school on Fridays. My teacher, Mrs. Jones, was the leading pianist in town, wife of McKinley, and mother of Edwina. They lived on the top floor of the first two-family apartment house on the street. They subsequently moved to South Huntington, and I was seldom able to have someone accompany me. So after three years, I took no more piano lessons, but the basics remained with me.

As usual, when the fire siren went off at eleven o'clock in the morning on November 11, all motion stopped to honor veterans of foreign wars. Since we celebrated Daddy's birthday on November 7, my mother was up one day and down the next, venting about her disgust and anger at the injustice of our men who chose to fight for democracy under the flag of France because the USA United States would not accept them—just as her grandmother and mother felt when Mosses Smith went to fight with the Massachusetts Volunteer Group in the Civil War.

I began to understand why Mom and Helen were angry and at each other so often. Before this enlightenment, I ran outside or hid anywhere, suck my thumb, and wait for the storm to blow over. Now whenever the scene became "heated," I put in my two cents. "I'll do it—let's do it, Helen." That seemed to blow the storm over. I think this was the beginning of my independent self. I believed it was triggered by the many friends and teachers who noted their thoughts in a beautiful autograph book given to me by Mom at Christmas, 1933. It was beige leather with a lock. Something of my own—personal and private!

From Helen, I learned about the lives of most "colored" people in the songs from Billie Holiday's "Strange Fruit" to the KKK. However, close to home, one night, Mom gathered us close in the darkened back parlor to show us the flame and smoke from a cross burning several streets over. She said that it was because "they" didn't realize that the woman was "colored" but could pass for white as many did—even from our own family.

Another enlightening experience came on our way to Girl Reserves meeting. One of the cousins said, "We'll get her—let's go."

So we ran, and I asked, "Who? What's happening?"

Laura said, "That kid called us niggers, and we're going to get her." She was slapped by each of her high-school mates and sent off howling. I later learned that she was another sister to a classmate of mine. They were dark Southern Italian and didn't care to be reminded of their heritage by "niggers."

I missed my friend Vera. Her family moved to Northport, Long Island, so I only got to see her during the summer at the Republicans' family picnic at

Sunken Meadow Beach, Long Island, and at the Sunday school picnics at Islip Hecksher State Park, always the first Thursday in August.

Cousin Bob was involved in the theater group at high school, and we were able to go to all the productions. I became hooked on theater. When the families gathered at our house on Sundays, with the encouragement of Bob, Buddy, and sometimes Vera if she was visiting her uncle and Edeline, we hung an old sheet from the clothesline and performed anything from fairy tales to poetry readings. We became so professional. We cleared the barn and ordered the grown-ups to bring their own chairs and pennies (we sold lemonade).

Bob graduated and went to live with his aunt in New York and majored in theater at City College. He later joined Work Progress Administration (WPA) theater group with Ossie Davis, Ruby Dee, and Canada Lee.

Cousin Ella refused to go to Huntington High—she didn't want to be in contact with classmates from families that Aunt Evie (her mother) worked for— so she graduated from South Huntington High. She and Helen were very close. She, as Girl Reserves leader, took the group to New York City for "exposure." They had a great night at the Renaissance ballroom while we "younger girls" were given a bag of jelly beans and a can of soda, and were stashed in a YWCA room listening to the Jimmy Lunceford Band playing next door in the ballroom.

Helen's graduation party was on the beach at Halesite, with cousins and friends attending. No one was in the water, and, as darkness set in, couples disappeared among the bushes. Helen refused the scholarship to Howard University, choosing to continue work as a "mother's helper" rather than go to the "separate but equal" South, away from family as she told me.

That summer for me was more trips to the library (unescorted now) and freedom to visit neighborhood cousins and friends. As I turned thirteen, in August of 1936, my curiosity about the people grew by leaps and bounds.

Remember the tea kettle.
It is always up to its neck
In hot water, yet it still sings!
—Anonymous

CHAPTER 3

THE SCHOLAR

In January 1937, I entered Huntington High School, taking classes in English, literature, accounting, typing, shorthand, history, and field hockey. I reveled in every minute of school. The result was that I was inducted into the honor's society ARISTA. Of course, our history teacher, Miss Gilbert, really socked it to me by announcing, "Your mother was an outstanding student, as well as your sister—I expect no less of you."

Arista

At home, I continued to collect poems, practice lessons and choir songs for church, and sew. That summer, Naomi, Laura, and I went to Fern Rock Camp, the YWCA camp located in Bear Mountain. I was overjoyed—as opposed to Naomi and Laura who hated every minute, as they told me over the years. "You went along with all that craziness—Pioneer Day, Indian Day, swimming, and horseback riding." I recaptured the joy and fun of camping in June of 1943, before leaving Long Island.

In the fall, while I was browsing through the Montgomery Ward catalog, I came upon a teal-blue winter coat with a princess style mink collar that was meant for me. As Mom ironed nurse's uniforms, she gently but firmly stated that she couldn't afford the coat, but I could earn the money by running errands, babysitting, or helping someone clean. *Wow.* That set me off on the work-save path. I used the bookkeeping forms from Mr. Higlee's class to begin my own personal budget and learned when and how you "rob Peter to pay Paul." I learned so much about the habits of the people I worked for, my family members, and friends. For instance, I spent several days with my cousin Rose, who was the same age but was an only child who lived with her mother, three aunts, an uncle, and her grandmother. My mother asked me to be friends with Rose at her mother's request, as she was just beginning to "be a girl," The family lived on Turkey Hill in Cold Spring Harbor and was the personal laundry and chauffeur for the Jones family.

I accompanied Rose to her one-room schoolhouse near the fish hatchery on Route 25A, and we spent hours talking and sharing on the lawn between the rows of sheets drying on the clotheslines. She felt alone at home and doubly so at school, being the only "colored" student—even though she was treated well in both arenas and was spoiled at home. At church and Sunday school, she wasn't allowed to mingle with the rest of her cousins because we freely mingled with all the other Sunday school attendees and participated in religious plays and young people's department functions—a Tom Thumb wedding, in which my brother George was the groom and a chubby, freckle-faced girl, Barbara, was the bride. We helped and participated in some way, but Rose was not allowed to. When I asked mom why cousin Grace wouldn't allow Rose to mingle, she said, "They don't want her to grow up too fast—they want her to finish school and go on to college."

I didn't understand because Helen could have gone to college; a couple of her friends went, and if I had the chance, I would go too, but we mingled. There was no further discussion.

While babysitting for Anglo-Saxon families, I learned that their lives revolved around Wall Street, land acquisition, and preservation of English-German royalty values. While helping my Jewish neighbors, I learned why the various holidays were sacred and why they separated dairy and meat dishes, cookware, ovens, and so forth. I listened to these families talk about "business in the Station, but not in the village"—not realizing the full impact until much later in college.

My first crush, Sonny, was overwhelming. Sonny met me at the movies and walked home with me. We were allowed to sit in the back parlor on the couch that faced the dining room where Mom was always ironing clothes. Sonny and I likened our affection to one another to the historic relationships found in our huge picture Bible—Adam and Eve, David and Bathsheba, and so forth. The pages were interspaced by family notes regarding births and deaths.

Another physical awakening came at a birthday party for cousin Laura that we attended. Billy monopolized my time, and I couldn't get any distance between his hot panting breath, kisses, and attempts at dancing until Maynard broke it up by saying, "Helen is ready to go, and I promised Miss Clara I'd see you both home in the car with Louis."

Bill and Florence

I asked Helen, "Is that what all boys do?"

She said, "Yes. You have to push or slap them to get away."

I settled into my schoolwork. I wrote an A+ account of "the effects of the storm of '38"—a hurricane on the north shore of Long Island—which closed the schools.

During the spring and summer of '39, while I absorbed jazz, as I had the classics over the years, I danced every chance I had. The theater had Friday-night Lindy hop competitions, and at times, in the gym at school, we taught anyone who was interested. At the annual Sunday-school picnic at Heckscher Park in Islip, we had numerous dance competitions where jitterbug enthusiasts performed for the picnic crowd.

The preparation for this picnic started in late spring. Mom assembled the makings for root beer, and my job was to hold the bottles as she capped them. The boys stored them in the cellar until August. The Bartlett pears were picked and stored, or else the tree would be stripped by the time we returned from the picnic. Cupcakes, cookies, baked chicken, tomatoes, and potato salad were all packed and ready for the day.

January 1940 was to be my last semester in high school, as I had earned more than enough credits to graduate in June. At sixteen, what was I to do? That spring, I watched the band practice. *Who was that guy playing the horn?* The next thing I knew, he also sang in the choir and attended Bible class and offered to walk home with me.

At graduation, the history teacher noticed that my last grade had slipped. What happened? I had fallen in love.

The graduation party at my home was wonderful.

*There is no danger of developing
eyestrain from looking on the
bright side of things.*
—Anonymous

CHAPTER 4

FROM THE HELPER...
TO THE HEALER

In the summer of 1940, I worked seven days a week between babysitting and washing dishes at large restaurants and acting as an attendant at a multimillionaire's home wedding reception. Later, I was a sleep-in helper for a family of four, summering at Lloyd Neck and accompanying them back to Brooklyn as school resumed for their girls. Away from home, I became more aware of the world to understand myself in terms of the poetry I kept in my scrapbook and the history of the people around me—especially the Jewish families on Church Street, who must be "terrified" by the events happening in Europe.

A viral infection took me back home to Huntington in December and under Dr. Granger's care for two months.

Good things were happening too. The claim of "master race" was dashed by our African American Jesse Owens at the Olympics and Joe Louis in the boxing ring. There was A. Phillips Randolph's march on Washington. President Roosevelt was pushed to sign Executive Order 8802, the first meaningful Fair Employment Act that opened the armed forces beyond the draft and forced any business or organization receiving federal funds to hire qualified "negroes." We were feeling joyous about future prospects.

My current days were spent waitressing morning and noon at Otelia's Tea Room, and my nights were spent there dancing to jukebox jazz. Weekends were spent at the local park—at football games where my friends and Frazier boys were playing—followed by socializing and dancing at the Watervliet social room at the Veterans of Foreign Wars (VFW) post in Amityville.

Bill Frazier and I were becoming close, and I was aware of his disappointment at being rejected for service in the armed forces. He had gone to the city to volunteer at the recruitment center, but when I saw him that evening, he was quiet and angry—"What does having flat feet have to do with service?" I agreed with the question but went on with planning our weekend fun.

I took employment as full-time "help" with a young family of three whose generational family was known to our Johnson ancestors. My mother and her siblings were more than satisfied. With the transitional half-day Thursday and all-day Sundays free, I planned with care to attend Saturday night dances wherever. I slept at home, and, for the half-day Thursday, I explored Nassau County via foot and bus.

I met Thelma walking her two-year-old charge. We exchanged information about our hometowns and decided that we wanted some of the same things—a place of our own, to know what each county had to offer, and to get to New York City often.

I'll never forget how excited she was on our first Sunday outing—two carloads of hysterically, hilarious teens exploring the Suffolk County parks from Huntington to South Hampton to the lighthouse. In turn, she took me through the Nassau County she was accustomed to—especially Glen Cove and Hempstead. Our working locations were "gated communities" in Manhasset on Route 25A near golf and tennis clubs. The nearest black restaurant was in Great Neck.

My friend Vera let me know of the New York State tests for clerical staff to be given in Mineola. Then Grumman Aircraft advertised for applicants interested in draftsmen traineeship prior to employment at the aircraft plant at Bethpage. I applied and enjoyed the training, and then being hired and partnered with Juanita to rivet the wings on the F6 fighter planes. It was a whole new world. Standard dress was blue coveralls and yellow-and-blue scarf. I took the bus to the plant at six in the morning, and the five fifteen bus home. The money, which I turned over to mom, was unbelievable. I kept just transportation and fun money.

Whenever I frequented the Tea Room for jazz and dancing, Howard was allowed to be there only until nine o'clock. At fifteen, he was a musician, the major drummer in the high-school band. Since "home" was across the street and a half block from New York Avenue, and everybody was "family," it was a safe community.

However, we all knew that every Friday night Connie in apartment three on Church Street was subjected to the rage of her weekend alcoholic husband, George. My concern was for their two year old, Cookie. He was so cute. So I told Mom that I was afraid for Cookie and would bring him to our house. She said it was OK. So for several Fridays, we had three boys in the house. George really enjoyed him too.

Cookie

Several times I was asked and consented to hostess at Mitchell Air Force Base USO Canteens in Hempstead.

That fall, Bill was drafted. We became engaged, and off he went to Camp Upton. Naomi and Walter married, and I was her maid of honor.

Meanwhile, I convinced my sister Helen and cousin Ella to take the Grumman draftsmanship-trainee program. Helen got a position at Grumman Beth Page, and Ella went to Farmingdale Republic Aircraft. Although Thelma didn't make the draftsmanship class, we continued our weekend fun times either in Huntington or Glen Cove.

Donny, one of my brother's closest friends, was rejected from service and the draft, and he was the only one of the available gang who had a car. So we women paid for gas and food in exchange for being chauffeured by our despondent comrade.

Despite the rationing of some foods (butter, sugar, etc.) and shoes, the holidays of 1942 were the best for us, with weekly checks that averaged more than a month of previous dollars.

Pictures and letters from Bill, who was assigned to the 369th Division at Fort Huachuca, Arizona, were grounding for me. Since becoming a part of the large workforce at Grumman's, I had few friends. Continuing to be a part of keeping our old friends together was somehow powerful—it was a way for me to have a sense of more control.

Bill came home on furlough suggesting we marry before he was sent overseas. This was on February 11, 1943. I said OK. We had to get the town clerk, whom we knew, to open the town hall. Bill got the license while I bought a dress. Bill was unable to get our AME minister but found the local Baptist reverend. We were married by seven in the evening on February 12 with nephew Charles and his wife Kate standing with us. The next evening, Bill left for Fort Huachuca.

I prepared for church on Sunday but changed my mind when I thought back to Friday when our pastor was not obliging toward our marriage. I went dancing on Sunday night, and then was off to work as usual on Monday. I couldn't believe how tedious the process of name changing could be at work and at the town hall for social security.

While I was at home, my brother George asked, "Why did you marry him?" Helen smiled and agreed with him. Howard and mom said nothing. I had no thought what my father might be thinking or his opinion about anything, since the only message Mom brought back from her weekly visit with him was that he asked about us and that he commented on any pictures she showed him and identified the who, when, and where of the occasion.

I was totally into "me"—feeling very grown, righteous, untouchable, powerful, and in control.

In March of 1943, I received a letter from New York State Taxation and Finance informing me that I had passed the junior-clerk exam and requested my response to a position. There was no question in my mind about accepting as I told Mom and Helen. I mailed the response and prepared to buy a bedroom set, as instructed by my husband, to place in the designated converted front parlor as he and mom had agreed. Well this was something to discuss. When did those two make that decision? Where was I? Helen laughed and said, "They really got you."

Back at work at the plant, I told Juanita about my over-the-holiday wedding and my acceptance of a clerical job with the state. She was supportive in terms of discussing my feelings about it and getting my reasoning for challenging my immediate family's apparent opposition.

I learned to smoke while on the job—it was the one legal way to take a break—so Juanita and I retreated to the cafeteria to talk and puff. As much as I felt in control, Mom let me know in no uncertain terms that I wasn't.

One Saturday night, New York Avenue and Church Street was teeming with young and old undrafted, drinking males and we sisters ready to dance at the Tea Room or wherever. Mom approached me as I was discussing where we were going and who was driving. She said, "You're married now and need to be at home." The gang separated. I went to the Tea Room and sang along with the orchestra. I heard her and understood the ethics, standard, and family pride behind her statement, and the next day after church, I told her that I wasn't pairing off with anyone. I was with the usual group minus Bill, Maynard, and Walter.

In early May, I received a letter of appointment as junior clerk in the Department of Tax and Finance. I was to meet with Commissioner Berinstein at the New York City office on Church Street for an interview prior to a July 15 appointment. I was overjoyed and in a daze, dressed in my Easter brown suit and yellow ruffled blouse. I took George and Howard with me and settled them in a movie theater close to Center Street office while I attended my interview. I was so confident, repeating my "Child of God" affirmation. The commissioner was visibly perplexed and thrown off guard by a nineteen-year-old Negro female leaving a job at Grumman's for a clerical position in upstate New York. As I recall, the interview lasted more than two hours! When I picked up George and Howard, they had seen the movie almost twice. On our train ride back, I described the meeting with the tax commissioner and let them know that I'd be going to Albany on July 15. We talked about them visiting and what there was to do up there where they had all that snow.

I later received support for my decision from Dr. Granger who, knowing my childhood ailments, quickly assured the family, especially Mom, that the drier climate was better for me. Also, the trains ran both ways. I've used this logic over the years, trying to encourage relatives to visit.

June 28 found Juanita and me at Fern Rock Camps reviewing our short work and friendship time together. I would work until Friday, July 9, and then take several days to pack—pajamas, underwear, three blouses, ration book, scrapbook, photos, weekly readers, Sunday-school cards, and mini Bible. Then I said my good-byes and headed out. I had written to Bill refusing to join him in Fort Huachuca, although I missed him terribly.

The letter I wrote from Fern Rock crossed his letter, informing me that he had a four-day furlough and would be home July 17 before shipping out to the Philippines.

My good-byes to mom, Helen, Howard, and George were painful, but upbeat. I phoned, wrote, and came home often. The Sunday and beach gang wished me well, and, on a fog-fringed Thursday morning at five thirty, I left to walk to the train station. On my way, I heard someone say, "We'd better hurry." It was cousin Dorothy with her bag to go with me to Albany, not just going as far as Jamaica, Queens, or New York City as we often had to meet cousin Bob or any of Dorothy's latest boyfriends. She said, "Ready to go? We'll miss our connection to Albany." Wow!

In later years, I imagined my mother and her sister, my Aunt Floss, Dorothy's mother, debating the pros and cons of this move, knowing the total disapproval of women leaving home without their husbands. Were they partially soothed by the two of us?

We made our connection because the Lake Shore Limited was late leaving Penn Station. However, we arrived in Albany at one fifteen instead of at twelve thirty. My appointment was at one. Dorothy said, "You go ahead. I'll find us a room and take care of our bags."

I asked directions to the Alfred E. Smith State Office Building and a traveler's aide representative said, "Out the door and up the hill to the tallest gray building." So, in my Easter outfit, brown-and-white saddle shoes, I walked up the hill to the city hall carillon bells playing "Amazing Grace" and entered the state office building. I found Miss Gaffney, chief of files, to whom I had been directed and apologized for being late. To the surprise of a superior, I was assigned to a unit of the income tax files, as opposed to being a part of the "downstate" contingent assigned to the motor vehicle unit housed outside of the "government downtown area" (the Capital building, state education building, and Alfred E. Smith state office building) in a facility in the western part of the city.

After fingerprinting and receipt of numerous forms to sign (tax, retirement, insurance, health, and responsibility as a government employee), I was schooled about my benefits with vacation, sick leave, smoking-break periods, lunch hour, holidays, special days such as Christmas shopping (time allowance of one day) and Saratoga track (one day), and payday (first and fifteenth of each month). I was also given an organizational chart of the New York State Department of Tax and Finance that listed the commissioner's name and showed the main and regional offices with the directors' names.

After a tour of the department, which occupied three floors, my unit supervisor, Eva Murray, introduced me to three others: her assistant, Bessie, and two other senior file clerks, E. B. and Eleanor Whaleon. The junior clerks' desks faced each other. My partner was a well-dressed, medium-height, curly-headed strawberry blonde who sported the largest diamond ring I had ever seen in my life. My partner, M. C., was so welcoming and not patronizing. She wanted to know where I was from, and then told me all about herself. She was also new that day, along also with Joe Flannery, who was a vet of WWI, and a woman who was recently deported from China. She was an American by birth but had lived there most of her life; she had to leave during this period of antiforeigner policy by the Chinese government. By the time we "clocked out," my head was spinning, my heart was light, and a prayer of thanksgiving was on my lips.

I met Dorothy outside. She was sunning herself on the steps of the building. She had no suitcase, only a local newspaper in hand and a big smile. "We've got a room two blocks from here—Mrs. Oliver's rooming house on Spring Street—near the grocery stores, a restaurant, and a library."

It's friends who make
This desert world
To blossom as the rose;
Strew flowers o'er our
Rugged path,
Pour sunshine o'er
Our woes.
—Anonymous

CHAPTER 5

SECTION I UNIT; INCOME TAX 1946

This was the beginning of my adult life. While I was at work on Friday, cousin Dorothy went job hunting and successfully gained employment at Williams Press in Menands. We celebrated by purchasing a bucket of spaghetti and meatballs for fifty cents from the take-out restaurant on Lark and Central. The second floor housed a psychic who held readings from three to ten o'clock, Monday to Friday. I visited her later in the year.

Our room at Mrs. Oliver's was on the top floor of her two storied, A-shaped wooden home on Spring Street. Mrs. Oliver, a small, feisty African American widow, shared the house with her unmarried son George. An older married son lived away from Albany and was only seen at church on Sundays. Mrs. Oliver prepared dinner for us that Friday night, complete with full linen, crystal, and silver place settings. Were we ever impressed, having only witnessed this opulence as we "helped" various families on Long Island. Small portions of chicken, mashed potatoes, string beans, apple pie, and tea were served as she simultaneously proceeded to give us rules, regulations, and expectations relative to our rental and conduct in the home and community. Attendance at Bethel AME Church was expected, and she was overjoyed and assured when I pointed out our AME affiliation. She raved over the names of "the good Albany families," listing the two (Felton and Freeman-Stroud) I met during orientation at the "files." She spoke of the places that were off-limits to good people, like the south-end red-light district. Did we understand what that was all about? Oh yeah.

There were four movie houses nearby—three in town and one in the South End, a Booker T. Washington community center where basketball games, dances, and teas were held. Her club sponsored many of these activities.

By the time we helped her and George clean up from dinner, we were exhausted and only wanted that top floor nine-by-twelve room with double bed and small dresser. There was a toilet and sink down the hall, which we shared with George. We later discovered that this wasn't the only space we shared with George. He had bored a peephole between the rooms, giving him a view to our every move. We notified Mrs. Oliver.

Before Dorothy left in September to meet her brother and "pen pal" Mayo Clarke at the naval base in Great Lakes, we spent every evening and weekend exploring Albany—the good and the bad. My first paycheck was spent on some needed appropriate clothes, and then, receiving an allotment, I was able to open a bank account.

I received a surprise visit from Bill, who found me at Big Charles, a jukebox bar located in the South End. Our letters had crossed in the mail—mine informing him of my Albany address, his letting me know of his furlough prior to overseas duty. Needless to say, he had a bad experience arriving in Huntington and being told with gleeful satisfaction by some, "She's gone, boy." However, when he came to Albany, he knew where to find me—wherever there was music and dancing, if not at the rooming house.

Unable to convince me to return to Fort Huachuca, Arizona with him to see him off to wherever, Bill left after two days. He called from the base, informing me that I would have been there less than twenty-four hours before he was shipped off to parts unknown.

I was thrilled and excited to be working in a permanent state clerical position and that I would be able to take exams for promotions. I was on top of the world. I was amazed to learn that one of the "colored" clerks was a graduate of Howard University. Working beside her with only my high-school degree made me want to question her about the rest of the whole crew, both white and "colored," in the department. Were they all college and business school graduates? Meanwhile, while alphabetically sorting two-and-one-half-foot file trays of individual W-2 forms that would eventually be attached to matching tax returns prior to the actual manual filing of both, desk partners got acquainted and exchanged home, school, work, and war stories as well as office gossip about our supervisors and the auditors upstairs. While the filers were 99 percent Irish females from the chief of files down to the principals and clerks, the auditors upstairs were 99 percent males with two African American males, one mixed Indian and African American, and two females. The balance consisted of Irish and Jewish males.

Income tax-adult life

Monday mornings, upon entering our section, we were quite aware of the many "lost weekends" as our supervisors drank their coffee, puffed cigarettes, and distributed work with shaky hands. By midweek, all was calm again.

I only experienced one negative interaction with supervisor E. M. One Monday morning shortly after my assignment, I asked for a stapler to attach similar W-2 forms as I caught them by similar name and social security number. She said that was not my job; it would slow up the work and duplicates would be caught later on. Her snapping prompted an immediate loud response from me. "When I have been here as long as you have, I'll be much further along than you are." I was good at my filing job—excellent at tracking down files to match incoming correspondence, following the audit trail on old files in order to process the checks, and marching upstairs to confront auditors who claimed to have returned files and demanding that they go through the stacks of files on their desks as well as their "special drawers."

From July 1943 until April 1945, the employee ratio remained the same. I became well acquainted with Helen Stroud, Alfaretta Noble, and Estelle Felton—each one of us assigned to different units. Helen and I shared common war stories, except that she had a seven-year-old girl and was a native Albanian. We all attended the same church, and they were members of the McLawton Club that Mrs. Oliver had spoken about. I shared with them my Aunt Evie's Phyllis Wheatly Club in Huntington, which was also a part of Empire State Federation and National Association of Colored Women's Club.

Helen Freeland

Fortunately, Mrs. Byrd, who lived two doors from the Olivers, offered me a much nicer room. So in September, Dorothy and I moved. While she made several unexpected trips back home, I busied myself fixing up our new space before she left permanently for Great Lakes Naval base where her brother Buddy and pen pal (and future husband) Mayo Clarke were stationed. With desk bookcase and radio to hear the weekly "Town Hall Meetings" broadcast from Lincoln Center in New York, I was living. However, one afternoon at my desk in the office, tears ran down my cheeks. My desk partner was away, and I just felt bad.

I wanted to go home. That evening, I was on my way, smelling the salty air of Long Island.

Satisfied, my world settled in Albany and in the immediate neighborhood of Washington Avenue, State Street, and Lark Street—downtown Peal Street where Saturday shoppers were dressed to the nines in white glove and hats. And Sunday church was the same. Ethylene T. shared a room at Mrs. Byrd's, as did a wealthy, elegant, fabulous and nearly blind elderly woman, and there was also Mrs. Ridgeway, who was finally rescued by relatives when we found her eating moldy food. All of us shared the kitchen facilities, and when we discovered Mrs. Ridgeway's problems, we felt guilty for not being more attentive. Bless Mrs. Byrd who assured us that it was more her responsibility than ours. Of course Mr. Byrd, the quiet, sly dandy from the European front was "glad to see her go." I always thought she was able to hear, or perhaps see, him slinking past her room to get to Ethylene.

When Ethylene left Albany on a job transfer to New York City, I didn't feel comfortable alone upstairs in that lovely house. While discussing the issue with my friend Helen, she suggested that I might want to bunk with her and her daughters while looking for an apartment. The war was coming to a close and I'd need an apartment similar to hers to prepare for my husband's return, which sounded good to me. From Spring Street to Orange Street to Northern Boulevard, in 1945, I felt really at home. Helen's godmother, Mayme Hoyt, babysat Little Helen upon her return from school and prepared supper for us all.

On the job, more employees came in. It was quite a diverse group. More local African Americans spread out to each section, with Polish and Italian girls completing the workforce. Yes, there were individual racial tensions—some acknowledged and dealt with person-to-person. Repeated problems were handled by the chief by separating conflicting personalities by location or unit reassignment. One worker, unable to work beside "a nigger," was reassigned to the newly separated department of Motor Vehicles.

The people on our floor were Albanian: Martha Ford and her sister Minetta from Schenectady; Helen S.; Isa Mae; Gladys Dukes; and Charles Epps, only one of three males on the entire floor, along with Joe Flaunery, a vet of WWI and a former male employed in the partnership section of the files whose supervisor was Alfaretta Miller. Martha Merietto, Gladys, Helen, and I soon found common ground over a game of pinochle on our lunch hour.

The supervisory task force added a senior clerk, Eleanor Whalen, another grand Irish girl who was young and a lot of fun. She and her boyfriend, who could not divorce his institutionalized wife for religious reasons, just enjoyed themselves and the world as it was. She and I became quite close as I took promotional exams for both senior file clerk and senior clerk. We talked about the difference between them in terms of job placements, opportunities, and salary. Eventually, these exams were merged under job duties that included knowledge and skills of math, English, supervision, and the exam for entry-level clerks.

I also discovered Capital Arena, which held weekly boxing events and, periodically, a solo musician. I heard that Nat "King" Cole would be presented—so naturally I made my way to see him. The early-day, thin, gaunt, acne-faced Nat Cole mastering the piano and belting out songs that we would eventually sing for generations was quite a treat.

I knew more people at church and in the Arbor Hill community. My friend Helen and others encouraged me in joining the Lawton Club, which enlarged my social network as well as connecting with my aunts back in Huntington. I was surprised to know that New York City and Long Island were as distant and unknown as California or Europe to most of these new friends.

One weekend I took Helen to meet my relatives, and, while in New York City, we strolled the avenue but were unable to visit the Empire State Building as an airplane drove into the tower. Helen was hooked on New York City. Over the years, we never missed an opening of a Broadway musical.

I saw an ad for an apartment on First Street, and, according to my native Albanian friend Helen Stroud, this was worth pursuing. It was four bedrooms with a back porch on the top floor of a three-apartment complex. The owner had a barbershop on the corner of Clinton Avenue and Hawk Street. Mr. C. gladly rented it to me with a warning, "Pay no attention to the first floor and basement tenants. This is my property. If they don't like you, they can leave." I understood totally, having hit some prejudice while shopping on Lark Street and in downtown Albany.

After seeing the apartment, I was overjoyed. The location enabled me to walk to work via the bridge or steps, visit Helen on Orange Street, and attend the movies on upper Clinton Avenue (the Paramount). Arbor Hill seemed to be the choice neighborhood. To the east, Ten Broeck Street with its many brownstones, the old Catholic church, and historical Ten Broeck Mansion. African Americans owned their homes in Arbor Hill. Many were entrepreneurs and beauticians, barbers, restaurant owners, bar and grill owners, general contractors, shoeshine or stationery storeowners, or cleaners and driers.

The Arbor Hill Community Center or Booker T. Washington Center (at that time) along with Baptist churches on the hill was the center of activities for adults as well as children. However, the "old" Albany people went to Israel AME Church across town, except for the several families who attended the Catholic Church or the Episcopal Church at Swan Street, near Washington Avenue.

On Broadway, downtown from Arbor Hill, were several nightclubs owned by families living on First and Second Streets in Arbor Hill: Three Sisters or the Rings, Richards, and Dorsey's. What a feast for this naturally curious, exploring child—still somewhat naïve despite being courageous and constantly believing in good. I became friends with the Gibbons family: Tess, Dot, and brother Algie who was serving in the marines at that time. As often as his sisters sent letters, I enclosed a note. Mr. Gibbons had been a professional boxer in the West Indies and Mrs. Gibbons was a nice gentle lady—very much like my mother and aunts. What a wonderful world—shopping for curtains and looking at furniture.

I was up at seven, worked until five, went to the apartment to do some cleaning, and then went home for dinner, to talk with both Helens, and go to bed. One evening, I decided to go straight home. As I got in, I received a phone call from my mother informing me of my sister's attempted suicide.

The following months were days and hours of confusion, uncertainty, responsibility, and decisions. There was little time for music and dancing. I made several trips home to get some understanding of Helen's problems and my mother's guidance on the situation, which came from the family doctor who pronounced my sister "mentally ill" and said there was little the family could do for her. I suggested that Helen could come to Albany with me. This was the real crisis for me, as I wrote Bill, informing him of the situation and questioning what this would mean to our marriage, having the family temporarily located in our apartment. Work was no problem—in fact, it provided the support and focus I needed to continue balancing demands, needs, and feelings at work, at home, the war. Only the mundane, monotonous work of the files allowed me to plan for home and family while pursuing a clerical career ladder.

I had no response from Bill month after month of daily watching Helen become psychotic, hallucinate, and hear voices coming from the radio as we listened to the bombing of Hiroshima and the cessation of the war in the Pacific front.

Mother and I took turns sleeping at night until Helen slipped by us one night and disappeared. We notified the police. She was finally safe at Albany Medical Center Hospital with a specific diagnosis of schizophrenia. Their recommendation was Hudson River Psych Center where she stayed for twenty-four years. The Red Cross offered no help to me in my search for Bill. My friends who had mates in the Pacific had heard from them acknowledging their eminent return. My work support group, which included these friends, kept me alive and focused while church sermons of "victory, faith, and better times ahead," I suppose, gave some help. I checked out every state exam posted for upgraded clerical positions with the knowledge that I could do that. By 1947, I had to gain only one more year of experience to be eligible.

At home, the brothers were out of school. One was off to Korea.

Mother spent time between Huntington and Albany, with biweekly stopping at Poughkeepsie, where I met her and visited Helen when she allowed us.

Unexpectedly, Bill called from Huntington. He was home and on his way to Albany. So my married life began. What a great time it was. Five or six couples sharing work and war experiences; weekdays on the job; weekends at home over food, drinks, and pinochle; and a night dancing to jazz music at Kettles on Swan Street. A. Harder with his sax, Mac McKinsley on the violin, and sometimes Fuller on piano. Later when N. Valenati opened his club in the south end, "The Gaity," Howard became the featured drummer. This band was on the road weekends for the many years thereafter.

Most of the men in our group were accepting of their career wives; however, Bill was not happy about my working. When the exam for senior file clerk was posted, I expressed my intention during a Friday night get-together, which later proved to be my undoing. I had never seen Bill so angry as he lashed out at me for not trusting him to support us. "Stay home, and, if we want extra money, we can have poker games on the weekend, sell dinners, and take a cut for the house." I was shocked and furious as well to think that he hadn't or wouldn't move into a better world than Woodhull Street—the other end of town where this was the way of life. He left for Huntington to cool off that weekend, while I tried to figure out what I needed to study for the exam in March 1948.

Meantime, at work, I was given excellent yearly evaluations for performing the most difficult searches to match incoming money and correspondence with the files and member partners to match their businesses and locating misplaced files. I soon learned that some difficult cases for the auditors were buried with other unrelated files. I gained the reputation of a "persistent competent worker." When the auditors saw me coming, most greeted me with knowing smiles. "OK, what have I got that you have something for?" One very persistent, talkative auditor, M. D., followed me over twenty years, and I met and worked with his daughter D., a nurse at CDPC, who was just as jolly and friendly as her dad.

In March 1948, on exam Saturday, I had been nursing Bill through his bout with pneumonia and was off for two hours to take the exam, leaving him in the care of my mother. He was quite unhappy. He said, "Don't leave me." He was on the mend. He had no his temperature, cough had lessened, and there was no sign of fluid.

I said, "I'll be back. This is our future."

I aced the exam in forty-five minutes. When I got back home, he said, "I'm glad you didn't go." According to my mother, he slept the whole time.

On the job, we who took the exam compared notes and felt very good about our performances. At our lunch-hour pinochle sessions, I informed the group about the various types of questions that were asked, and a couple said they wouldn't be bothered, being satisfied with just doing this filing. As it was, there were times I was ready to knock one of them into the files.

Eventually the exam results were posted, and we were notified by mail of our individual scores and standing. I aced the exam and waited for a canvass letter for a senior file clerk at my own section where there was an opening.

However, the summer of 1950 saw the birth of our daughter, Elaine. I took six months of leave and returned to work in November. I was told that because of the "preferred list" someone now occupied the position.

Persons on that list were senior file clerks in any State Department that had closed, reorganized, or combined staff positions. Also, several persons who had taken leave to go into armed services had returned to any offered, open state position. I was quite disappointed, but having the support of the chief of the files and my section principal eased the pain. Within six months, the person who had taken the position moved on, and I received my appointment as a first-line supervisor. However, I could hardly wait to get home to baby girl Elaine, my sweet baby who woke up talking and smiling every morning and was ready for some playtime with Bill and me.

Over the several years since getting the apartment, we temporarily hosted my brothers and their wives, and, later on, a domestic violence escapee from Huntington who was a relative, and more permanently, my mother who helped me through those especially difficult first nights with my newborn.

However, by the early fifties, life had settled down to work, family, an occasional night out for jazz and dance, church, and once-a-month McLawton Club meetings.

Some weekends our couples with babies met for picnics at Saratoga Lake, Lake George, or Thatcher Park or fishing along some available spot in Rensselaer. I felt that we really had the best of all worlds. With the freedom and money to enjoy our work and play, it seemed as though we epitomized the preacher's model of the abundant life. A more attractive first-floor apartment became available on lower First Street, and we moved in 1953. This area comprised of single-family and apartment houses, all owned by African American families. The area—Northern Boulevard, Ten Broeck Street, Colonie Street, lower Clinton Avenue to Sheridan Hollow—was a black family neighborhood community. It was also comprised of some old Albany people—a few transient State workers from New York City and domestics working for Albany's wealthiest.

Bill became the Boy Scout leader and I a den mother and Elaine the "princess" little sister of them all. So between work on Monday through Friday;

Saturday scouting, cleaning, and shopping; and Sunday Church, we seemed to be constantly busy with little time for real planning or discussions about ourselves. Neither of us wanted to compromise on my having work or his evening and weekend lifestyle of drinking and gambling. Neither understood or took the time to know what was important to the other or how we were brought up. I refused to be a stay-at-home wife and weekend "house party" hostess, while his attempt to study business courses under the GI Bill, which would lead to self-employment, was scrapped after a few months.

In 1955, we separated. I took a one-bedroom apartment on the second floor of Ten Broeck Street. My mother came up from Long Island and lived with me, although our regular childcare worker was more than willing to continue with a cut in her fee. I continued to take pride in my work and the friends I made along the way while looking for a house to buy.

I especially felt the wonder of a close relationship with another woman—the intimate sharing of opinions; theater; world events that impacted our lives; and racial issues, particularly on the job. I knew that the circle of women I encountered were proud of my position at work and had been supportive of my marriage—as a couple devoting time to scouting, church, and so on and with our need to my institutionalized sister.

While continuing with my church work, I had the opportunity to attend a four-day retreat for Protestant youth workers at Fond-du-Loc, Wisconsin. It seemed to be the healing I needed at that time. The four o'clock vespers and evening hilltop relaxation where the entire world was open sky. It was, at first, frightening, and then awesome. Each night I went back for more. That experience has continued with me through my travels; that aloneness meshing with the universe of God. I don't remember the bartender who "smashed our glasses." As Dorothy P. recalls, "I was in another world."

Upon my return home, my insurance agent notified me of the availability of a house for sale at 98 North Swan Street. It was a two-family home with central heating, and the second floor was currently rented. And I had just dipped into my savings for the retreat. My father had just partnered with his sister and bought a house in Huntington, so he wasn't able to help me and felt so badly about my separation.

I took a leave from club attendance and concentrated on Elaine's first year at school, exploring the beautiful Pruyn Library with her, swimming at Lincoln Park with her cousins, and joining the many activities at Arbor Hill Community Center as assistant Girl Scout leader.

Dad and his sister brought another house in Huntington. However, I was eventually able to cover the down payment before someone else did, and, on September 1, 1956, Mother, Elaine, and I moved in. Mom was adamant about not returning to Huntington, citing her choice to be close to her children, grandchildren, and new friends and easier access to visit Helen at Hudson River State Hospital.

I threw myself into work, feeling a freedom I hadn't felt since first coming to Albany in 1943. I guess it was more an aspect of being in control and making the right decisions—not all pleasant, as I had to evict the tenant under court order after finding two-plus inches of dog feces in the kitchen and on the back porch upstairs, in addition to their delay in paying rent. A friend suggested that instead of leaving the top apartment vacant, I use it as an extension of the family and bring a foster child in to accompany Elaine and my mother at home. Each one of us was comfortable with the idea, so by the time the social worker came to make the home family assessment, which determined that we were not in need of the thirteen dollars per week that would be provided to my mother, the deal was closed. The family eventually became Mom (Nana) to Elaine and the three foster children: Deb, Emily, and Kenny. With cousins around the corner on Clinton Avenue, north on Colonie Street, and across town on Myrtle Avenue in the south end, The Jackson-Frazier infiltration of Albany was established.

Both principal file clerk and principal clerk exams were posted, and I applied for both. The income tax department was expanding. There was talk of the necessity of expanding the four sections to five or six. The collection unit needed more space and, perhaps, a new building was needed just for tax. I encouraged relatives to take the exams, which they did, and, in 1960, on budget approval, the huge influx of the new, diverse file clerks had to be prepared for.

I received a promotion to principal file clerk as head of a new section with an assistant, a senior file clerk, two seniors, and thirty file clerks. Another major assignment was to plan the needed floor space at the new tax department campus site on Western Avenue.

I had nine to five work, and then motherhood from five to ten. Payday was newly legislated as every other Wednesday. The older girls, Elaine and Emily, met me at five thirty at the Grand Cash Market for heavy-duty grocery shopping, and then we took the bus home. The market on Swan Street was good for fresh fruit, vegetables, and interim necessities.

For three weeks in December, I attained extra Christmas money by sorting mail at the post office from five thirty to eleven thirty at night, with a fifteen-minute break at eight and Christmas Eve bargain shopping wherever with my sister-in-law.

Prior to Easter, weather permitting, we went window-shopping downtown after church and selected the best fashions for spring. On many Sundays, we took the girls with us to visit Aunt Helen—making a great picnic time, especially the year when two cars went to Poughkeepsie. The girls wore their matching jumper outfits, each having selected her own color. I like to think that these experience of "fun time" combined with sharing helped the girls to understand themselves and the responsibilities of women of different generations.

We took trips to Long Island to visit our relatives, trips to the mountain lakes after Saturday chores were done, and activities at the Arbor Hill Community Center.

While volunteering at Arbor Hill Community Center (where after school activities for the young were held: sports, cooking, Girl Scouts, sewing, and so forth, as well as adult groups including amateur theater), my resolve for further education resurfaced. SUNY had no part-time studies programming yet, so I applied to St. Rose. I was confident that my academic and honor-society credentials would guarantee acceptance, and the only possible problem would be the tuition payments. Much to my surprise, I was told that because I had not taken a physics course, they could not accept me, "Perhaps our brother school, Siena, might consider you." (Send this black woman to the white male college.)

After many days of deliberation (that I now call mediation), I called Siena and followed through with transcripts in hand to meet Mr. Curvans, the admissions director. He read the transcripts and references from teachers and tax supervisors, and then turned red and stomped out of the room, cursing under his breath. He returned with the admission papers, schedule of classes, and curriculum. He requested my willingness to take the upcoming GRE (graduate record exam) being given at the armory in Troy. That was no problem. "I would like to have you start classes as soon as possible," he said.

I aced the exam, the results of which he forwarded to his admissions counterparts at St. Rose, and I started Siena College part time in the June 1962 summer session in the evenings until all my classes were completed in 1968. My final tuition payment was in January 1969.

*The blossom cannot tell what
becomes of its odor, and no
man can tell what becomes
of his influence. . .*
—Anonymous

CHAPTER 6

WORK, FAMILY, AND COMMUNITY

The sixties were the most challenging on all fronts—home, community, and, especially, at work. My supervisory duties expanded with each promotion, yet I looked forward to each day. From first-line supervisor of twenty to fifty file clerks, I was promoted to principal head of a unit, supervising three first-line supervisors, one of whom was my assistant. During this time, Albany County Neighborhood Youth Corp trainees were placed within the department. I was asked to accept one young girl who seemed to be totally lost. Just being away from her south-end home base during the summer took empathy and time from all of us to help her overcome anxiety and fear.

Another experience that was gratifying was being asked to serve on a committee appointed by the civil service commissioner, Eras Poston. The mission was to examine various test questions for bias and compile data on diversity in all State departments by level of employment. The chair of the committee was Dr. Julian Parrish. There were several other members, but I recall being the lone female. Twenty years later, I had the opportunity to evaluate the outcome of this project, which documented numerous departments with no nonwhite employees, while three (corrections, mental hygiene, and motor vehicle) had several, all grade three and under.

Simultaneously, the State's progress was pushed in several other directions, one of which was to find how many out-of-state residents commuted daily to their New York City employment. I was asked to assemble a task force to purge the A to Z and report the results to the chief of files each morning. This was gratifying to me for the extra checks, as well as a chance to work closely with a few select clerks for one week from six to nine. My first island vacation and airlines flight set me up for future vacation goals.

Spurred on by the department head, I enrolled in training classes directed by the civil service department: supervision, case studies in supervision, work simplification, and public administration. After receiving my twenty-year pin and a merit award, I persuaded the chief of file clerks, in light of the more complex duties, which involved a tremendous volume of work and the necessity of some knowledge of Hispanic language and culture. New York State's tax-paying population was boosted by the postwar economy plus the Fair Employment Act. After a twenty-minute condescending, hurried session, the chief and I returned to our sixth floor, agreeing that top administration was indeed not interested in "preventing backlogs, fraudulent use of social security cards, inability to collect revenues, etc." In other words, "these issues aren't important now."

I settled down to my philosophy and Shakespeare courses at Siena, using lunch hours, evenings after the girls had retired for the night, and sometimes sharing my studies with them over the weekend. My mother was also schooled in English literature. So many times, it was round-table discussions.

Elaine received a scholarship award from the tax department, as well as her New York State Regents Award and was a National Honors' Scholar. Young foster sister D was studious and grew to become self-sufficient despite tough challenges. However, we joined a local church headed by two diverse pastors, both of whom had a family of early teens that afforded us more opportunities to be together—singing in the choir and directing Christmas pageants and other activities that we previously were not able to share.

Elaine

Our house was very full now, with my father having come for Thanksgiving '65 on a one-way ticket and deciding that he too wanted to be with his family and get to know the boys especially. What fun watching mother and father interact after we settled financial responsibilities. Now the three-generation Johnson-Jackson family was in Albany's North and South Ends. Further involvement of our children developed from the activities of the Center Players at Arbor Hill Community Center. I found the biweekly theatrical group stimulating, challenging, and fun. From this group, I not only developed several more long-term relationships, but also got a better understanding of myself.

The adult program director, who had an extensive, impressive background in community theater, built the group's confidence and skills to the level of preforming *A Streetcar Named Desire*—two public night performances in the auditorium of the junior high school. Both sisters-in-law were also involved in each production. We took second place at the Northeast One-Act Play festival in Springfield, Massachusetts, for our song-dance in an original musical by a local teacher-musician, "Love Knows No Season." I was not content in the role as the housewife Eunice Hubber in *Streetcar* but played it anyway.

However, in the one-act play, Four Hundred *Nights*, I was the court stenographer and was quite satisfied. The real joy was singing and dancing in "Love

Knows No Season." I had long discussions with several group members and concluded that yes, school was for me. Group settings and community activities stimulated and would be adventitious in my classroom.

In addition to the NAACP and M. C. Lawton Club community work, I eventually accepted my good friend Helen's plea to join the Links Inc. "You need us as much as we need you." So true. For instance, as a board member of council committee services, I was asked to sit on a committee to establish an urban league in Albany, which would take these various community issues to a group of our own "colored Negro black African Americans," as well as consciously directing pertinent information critical to the "other" boards. The most exciting and extensive involvement began when I was asked by an Albany Medical College task-force representative to attend a meeting at Dorsey's Café to explore the "community's interest in establishing a health center."

The middle and late sixties were a busy time for everyone who was alive and aware of the civil rights. Racial tension from country to community to family to school, newspapers, and even our individual experiences documented the various levels and degrees of conflict. We all reacted to the turmoil, which brought forth the old smothered feelings by declaring war and taking self-satisfying action on our own.

As the goodwill champions of civil rights from north and west met with southern groups, as diverse a group as NAACP met with the BAN (Black Action Now) to protest the lack of black men being hired to work on the South Mall project. In the classroom, unknowledgeable teachers were confronted by challenging facts from homeschooled students and church and temple leadership—some of their congregations supported the brothers and Martin Luther King.

I missed my companion John who had encouraged my return to school and awakened me to the need for a car, as transportation for the girls to their various teenage activities and for me as a means of relaxation. His promotion to assistant engineer forced him to locate to Westchester County. As a result, most of our time was spent on the phone, usually after ten at night, and together on an occasional Saturday or Sunday. I purchased my first car, "the gray ghost," an old Kaiser-Frazier, four-door sedan. It took us over the hills of Vermont in the fall and to Huntington in the summer until I traded it in for a Chrysler convertible, which thrilled the girls and cousins.

At home, the years between '67 and '69 were life-changing and challenging. Elaine received offers complete with scholarships from various colleges, and was recruited to be among an international diverse group to open the New York State University at Old Westbury. This called for her to work sometimes on campus and for me to restructure the budget to help support her. I had discussed moving to a location near the Harriman Campus where the new tax and finance building was located.

Elaine prom

Putting the Swan Street property up for sale proved emotionally difficult, as we all had invested so much in the house, including the garden and grape arbor in the back. However, after several fires were set on the front steps and Emily fell in love and didn't want to observe curfews, it was time to move out of the area, while continuing commitment to the various organizations. So the pride of hearing Elaine belting out Gershwin's "Summer Time" at the Palace Theatre class of '68 graduation overcame the anger and disappointment toward Bill for not attending as promised. Now Mom and Dad, Helen, Howard, George, friends, and neighbors were thrilled, along with the parents of her scholastic friends.

98 N. Swan Street

How ironic that she returned to the island I had fled from when I was nineteen. All parents must have some discussion with a child leaving home. One issue I stressed was that Suffolk County's minority population was most likely relatives, so she had to be careful dating. Debbie missed her big sister and Emily's leaving plus her aunt had introduced her to many cousins. She asked questions I couldn't answer and her aunt wouldn't, saying, "When you're older you can go to Philadelphia and perhaps track your mother down." We made several trips to settle Elaine, and, in August, I discovered that a friend's daughter was going to a private Protestant international high school. After discussion with Deb, I enrolled her in this highly academic school.

Elaine, Deb, Diane, Emily, and Linda

One evening, a phone call from John woke me up at nine thirty at night. At first, I couldn't believe him, but as old memories and situations surfaced, I became angry and hung up the phone with a resounding, "No. Sleep it off." He had related his "psychiatrist's recommendation that we come together for a session." John was told, "You feel threatened by your bride-to-be's success in passing exams. She now has another promotion. What has that to do with your feelings for her and plans for the future?"

John

I couldn't believe that a man who had been one of the strongest supporters of my getting a degree and moving to the top of the clerical-administration career ladder was acting as badly as my ex-husband had twenty years ago. We discussed this episode subsequently over the years, but I felt quite disappointed. As I got to know more career-minded women, I understood. It's the men's problem to work out.

Head Clerk

More often, I found satisfaction in my community and board work and was settled in mind about what '69 would be. The last prospective buyer for the Swan Street house was unable to get her bank clearance. Since I had completed my realtor and bank negotiations, I asked my brother George if he and his merged family would like to rent the house, with the rent going toward buying it. He was more than willing. I was overjoyed, and so it was.

The North Side Advisory Council (NAC), a community-staffed office, had begun the process of developing health care. The professional developer and staff were housed in a facility on Lark Street. One night, while directing a NAC meeting to discuss eligibility for health services at the center, I was verbally attacked. "You don't belong here. You talk white" Yes, I had moved from Arbor Hill, and I didn't speak "ghetto" or have a southern accent. I continued our session accepting my "shortcomings" and later turned in the decisions recorded by Judy Stewart who directed the NAC office. They subsequently developed a work board and Dorothy Paul volunteered as president. She later resigned from her State job to be assistant administrator of the center. Her work with Izetta Fisher, representing the Urban League, and the Albany Medical College backing provided the groundwork for the health center.

My graduation was near. I took the civil service technical and professional careers exams, and both resulted in numerous canvass letters offering grade-eighteen positions at mental-hygiene and correctional facilities. I had received my twenty-five-year service pin and a promotion to coordinator of income-tax files.

In recent years, I remembered having to demonstrate and explain—a real show-and-tell—the process by which New York State's income tax system functioned to a delegation of three Jordanians. One asked to meet others. "You know we are the same." There was nothing left to do but take him to the M. C. Lawton concert at the Institute of History and Art that evening. Several letters from various cities before his return helped him to understand that there was more than mileage separating a Jordanian from this American.

Mom visiting Helen

My response to the mental-hygiene canvasser was that I was not interested in State Hospital. When an opening became available at a community mental health facility, I would be available.

In the meantime, I completed all my Siena courses but couldn't officially graduate until all the tuition payments were completed. By January '69, I was looking for my second merit-award notification as well as being focused on a future professional position. I had received correspondence from mental hygiene acknowledging my work-location preference and assuring me that I would be notified relative to the possible Albany area site. In March '69, I received a letter requesting my response relative to definite interest and an interview for appointment.

Israel AME

I took a one-year leave of absence from tax and finance, went for the interview, and transferred to mental hygiene in April 1969.

I recalled the professor at Siena who cautioned me about accepting a position among professionals at a State mental-health facility. He stressed the hierarchy in the medical profession and their attitude toward nonmedical people, but I could return to tax and finance within a year.

Blessed is he who has found his work; let him ask no other blessedness, he has a work, a life purpose; he has found it and will follow it.
—Thomas Cartyle

CHAPTER 7

DEINSTITUTIONALIZATION— COMMUNITY PSYCHIATRY

According to civil service, I was now a psychiatric social worker trainee who found herself in the conference room of professionals—psychiatrists, psychologists, nurse practitioners, RNs, MSWs, the human resource director, and three secretaries. The center occupied the first floor of the mental-hygiene building on Holland Avenue. The "mobile geriatric team" was developed and had been in the community since the fall of '68. As the charge was for community mental-health services to cover a nine-county area, there was a tremendous amount of work to be done and relationships to develop on the foundations previously laid through political, organizational, medical, and personal contacts.

My assignment was with Psychiatrist Berkowitz's focus on Albany City and who, how. when, and where the community mental-health model would be relevant. However, for the first two months, I was expected to discuss my thoughts relevant to the experience at our weekly staff meetings. While the Albany City team leader and I shared our knowledge of the city and our personal lives. His file on the activities of "the brothers" (Leon Vandyke and Sam Dowell) surprised yet encouraged me to help him expand the potential of this unit.

The chief psychiatrist directed me, as a trainee, to have clinical social-work supervision weekly with B. D., who had graduated in the first SUNY Albany class of '68. At my first staff meeting, we were asked to give our names, professions, and counties. B. D. said, "Florence, what does coming into the middle class mean to you?"

SUNY Albany MSW Elaine & Florence

I said, "What do you mean by middle class? Money, or values like education and manners?"

There were red faces all around the room, and my team leader said, "Yes, Belle, define it for us all."

After the laughter, we got down to the business of planning for a community mental-health program with other health providers to this targeted population.

The community health center project for Albany's north end was a major priority along with getting the community to become knowledgeable of the Capital District Psychiatric Center (CDPC). I traveled to New York City, visiting Albert Einstein Clinic, the rehabilitation project of Dr. June Christmas, and Martin Luther King Community Mental Health Center to give me some background on the programming needs of the patients living in the community. I also paid weekly visits to Hudson River Safe Hospital (HRSH) to gather data around the number of people from the area who might be appropriate for resettlement, talking with those people, and reporting back to CDPC administration.

In the fall of 1969, the crisis erupted at Albany High. Some of the black male students came back to Albany High and told the black students that they weren't getting a complete literacy program. A riot broke out. Seeing that this type of crisis needed to be addressed by a community-based psychiatric service,

I requested permission to spend time at the school and with the parents and students involved. Permission was granted, and Dr. Young, Vernall Allen, and I started the United Black Parents Association.

Our negotiation with the school board, Dr. Hepinstal, and small groups with parents and students discussing alternatives led to my involvement with the establishment of the Street Academy under the pen of Sister Maryellen Harmon and the Urban League. I became first chairman of the board of Street Academy in September 1970.

I left CDPC to attend SUNY/A School of Social Welfare full time, following a six-week human relations seminar that I designed and conducted at CDPC for the staff. This diversity-seminar format consisted of three meetings, each featuring a community professional, followed by three staff meetings to evaluate the sessions where individual staff gave program input and CDPC's overall mission goals and obligations. I was congratulated and supported by administration and most of the professional staff. The exception was a male psychologist, who refused to attend the last session, saying, "I won't be told how to do my job." During our evaluation sessions, the director identified several open staff positions and encouraged our work with Office of Mental Retardation and Disability (OMRDD).

The exposé of cruel treatment of the children at Willow Brook, Staten Island, caused concern for the children in our nine-county upstate area. I remembered a clerk in my unit at the tax department who had been a medical assistant before relocating from Long Island to Schoharie County and recommended her for a possible position. I was asked to work with an OMRDD employee who was writing and illustrating guides for Head Start and kindergarten teachers, "What is a Family?" and "Who is Family?" I thought it was timely and appropriate, especially for the Albany City unit, but it wasn't accepted by the district.

Although I was a "full-time student" beginning in the fall of '70, my involvement with the developing community-health center and Albany County Mental Health Association necessitated weekly contact with Dr. Berkowitz at CDPC. He asked to attend the meetings between Albany Medical College MDs, administrative personnel, and NAC (Northside Advisory Council persons working toward service-area boundaries, staffing needs, relationships between current county health providers, state proposals, and overall diversity issues. Several meetings became heated or confrontational.

I made a home visit to one NAC member following a particularly heated meeting. We shared the feeling of "battle fatigue" but knew this must go on. One major concern she had was that the staff of the center would all be white. I pointed out that one major task for board community members was to identify potential staff to be hired, like Anona Joseph and Harriet Gibbons, who were staff persons at the program office on Lark Street as well as the United Black Parents, Urban League, churches, and organizations. Yes, it would be a lot of work, but did we want the health center to reflect the location and service area? Everybody had to do their parts. I shared my nonprofessional work and volunteer life with her, stressing the various occasions when I was the only black person. She later helped the male board members better focus on the importance of their roles.

At school, from September '70 to May '71, the basic social-work premise of person-to-person relationships seemed right up my alley. The challenges came from some facility interpretation and bias, along with several black students from Louisiana who were unable to tolerate the "white environment" and left after the first semester. I learned so much about myself as several papers were returned with, "Not enough of you in this," "What were you feeling?" and "Did you act from knowledge or intuition?" It was if I had been given permission to let it all hang out. The trick was when, where, with whom, and to what extent I let "me."

My friendship circle grew from each new setting. My first field placement was at Albany Home for Children, now Parsons Family and Children's Center. I joined a young male childcare worker's "Black Heritage Group," which was concerned with exposing the kids to black businesses, such as the barbershop for proper hair care, as well as exposing them to males who would get the boys to start thinking about what they wanted to be. Another contact, made as a result from filling the position at Street Academy, later started an alternative school in Roxbury, Massachusetts and wrote extensively about teaching to adolescents with special needs and curriculum development.

While full time at SUNY, I had many luncheons, seminars, appointments, and scheduled volunteer hours with Northside Advisory Council board members, interviewing prospective staff and CDPC staff. The blurring of needs and overlap of goals put my life in perfect synchronization. Community development class discussion resulted in the professor bartering with me, giving me a passing grade for an outline for the class final exam. CDPC asked me for introductions to several community organization members. Since the geriatric team had been in operation for over two years and the medical school (Albany Medical Center and Union College) were long-established institutions, what of their contacts? It was quite a revelation. How completely separate the professional establishment was from the community it supposedly served.

At home, Deb made friends with a few late-night alcohol and drug users and sometimes skipped school. We talked and argued, and she let me know "it was her life." Yes, but rules for living there were to be kept. I received a call from the owner of a resort that she was there with some not-so-nice people asking, "Can I bring her home?" She and I had quite a confrontation upon her arrival. Subsequently I called her caseworker, resulting in an all-around agreement that she attend a boarding school. It was particularly difficult for Mom and me to lose the last of our girls. We broke the news to Helen on our visit the following Sunday and to Elaine via phone. Elaine was quite upset but knew the drug crowd that Deb had been exposed to.

The spring of 1970 was overwhelming as I was asked to help CDPC with the curriculum development of a human-services course for mature returning students at Hudson Valley Community College. Our head nurse, Margaret Teabout, had outlined the proposal and wanted some "fill-in." Simultaneously, the CDPC administration was in the process of proposing a "career ladder" for its employees, and the Hudson Valley mature returning student program would, perhaps, be on the career path. By the end of the semester, I was happy to take two weeks to do nothing and being "away" before returning to CDPC for summer work.

The "mandated" day program for patients started at nine, although the "community room" kitchen facility was open to them from eight to find the free spirited at nine at night.

I arrived between eight and eight thirty in the morning to find the free-spirited, freedom-loving, cigarette-smoking young-at-heart adult patients singing and dancing to Sly and the Family Stone and The Isley Brother's "It's Your Thing." I never forgot the joyous expression on their faces or their willingness to prepare for community meetings with staff and discuss anything, question whatever, uninhibited and able to challenge staff as well as copatients.

This daily meeting was a real testing ground for the concept of a community psychiatry day-treatment program. Some staff, as well as defiant patients, shunned this open-sharing, confrontational, sensitive "what's happening" meeting as individuals related their ups and downs over the past twenty-four hours. Particularly highlighted were the patient-staff combinations that had responded to crises overnight. On-call staff might respond to a client in crisis and spend anywhere from a half hour to four hours, ending up with the client and staff further exploring the crisis with support in the community meeting the next day. Weekends were difficult.

From this meeting, clients were scheduled for small-group music therapy; rehab; special issues; family and couples' therapy; activities of daily living, such as shopping, cooking, cleaning, and soforth. They ate lunch out or in the cafeteria downstairs. Some had to go to clinics, DSS, and so forth.

I conducted socialization groups for the multicultural young adults on such topics as social conduct, restaurant manners, job fairs, and so forth. Our group increased due to the closing of Rome State School, the comparable upstate facility at Willow Brooks on Staten Island.

In April, Father Hubbard asked if I could sit in with a young man from New York City who would be conducting group sessions with recovering addicts in "Providence House" on South Pearl Street. After several sessions, we all agreed that I was not strong enough and I didn't have the time for more volunteer work.

By the spring of 1970, our patient population was growing along with the staff. Several social-work trainees and mental-health aides were brought on board. Although they were assigned to other units in Albany County, Rensselaer, Schenectady, and so forth, two became long-term friends.

I needed "fun time." One of the new mental-health trainees was Judy, known to Elaine and me from our church affiliations. As teenagers, her white Baptist groups often met with the diverse teams at Temple Baptist for Sunday roller-skating, Bible study, and so on. She and the other trainee, Janice, became immediate friends and both called on me as "Mother Hen." Elaine and Janice had functioned as sisters. Janice was the older one, and Judy was the "very young, unknowing one." So, although I no longer had the giggly, argumentative, competitive preadolescent girls coming into the bedroom on Saturday mornings to romp on the floor, I loved being with these almost adults while we planned our weekend.

Elaine needed encouragement and returned to Old Westbury. Janice left to pursue her degree at SUNY and Janice to remove herself from a domestic violent marriage. We all supported Mother as Dad was taken to the VA hospital after numerous transient ischemic attacks.

At CDPC, during the summer of '71, along with my assignments of morning community meetings, intakes, health-center liaison, and the supervision of two Hudson Valley students I had recruited, I was to have a psychologist from a Pennsylvania state prison accompany me as I visited families in the community.

A Haitian psychiatrist joined the staff of Albany City Unit. When he encountered a crisis situation with one of his clients that mandated a home visit, he called on me to accompany him. Delores Brown, MSW, was another staff person hired on the Rensselaer team. She and I became involved with organizing a black social workers' group on campus. She attended the National Association of Social Workers (NASW) conference, during which the black group caucused and united to separate from the national body. Cenie Williams, MSW, from New York City headed the group and spearheaded its operations for subsequent years, encouraging neighborhood daycare centers and health centers. Anyone who taught, preached, or cared for us could join the Black Social Workers.

Award presetation

I recall how excited and encouraging Helen was as we exchanged "What's been going on with you since last month." She wanted to know about Elaine, Deborah, and so forth; gave Mom her latest needlework needs and price; and closed off the visit with, "Don't work too hard. These people aren't nice." She was very much her own self and in control.

So we entered the fall of '71 at the school of social welfare, bringing an open mind but a sharply focused view of May '72 graduation for Elaine, myself, and the Hudson Valley student I had recruited. I served on the Minority Recruitment Committee and the Curriculum and Structure Committee and developed a course on the black family, presenting it at the marriage-counseling seminar at the request of Dr. Rooney. My field placement was at legal aid, in the family unit. My task was to determine if a group experience, in addition to legal service, might be helpful to the client in addition. One night a week, I was co-leader of this group, which became the model for legal aid's "Worry Workshop." Additionally, I met with the Friday Ministers Seminars, and workshop held at the legal-aid office.

Graduation '72

My statistics class presented a challenge until I submitted a proposal for community volunteers' board training to both my professor and the Albany Mental Health Association. Taking the maximum feasible participation theory of the commission, I got a high grade in the class, and the National Health Association was ready to fund the project. Had I not been so close to retirement, I would have accepted. I felt badly about the Albany Association not being able to convince the Feds that there were others willing to proceed with the grant. However, several years later, Father Young found someone to develop a volunteer training program and requested the use of my grant model. I said, "Of course."

Mental Hlth Drive Father Young, Dr. Alan Miller, Earnest Boyer

I realized that I would not be a part of this "cutting corners" and "killing two birds with one stone," so I discussed the issue of my being a student as well as an employee at CDPC. Meanwhile, the school requested student placement in the program with my supervising team, as other teams were not able to accommodate student social-work interns. CDPC administration and team leaders agreed with me, and I subsequently received a letter of regret from the school director of field education. This issue was further explored, and my position was reinforced by the knowledge that all faculty positions include "field-liaison commitment."

The home-front challenge came when I returned Helen to the hospital from a weekend home visit and the charge nurse told me, "Helen has been discharged."

"When? To whom? Where? Helen, did you know?"

Helen said she was unaware of her discharge—just that her weekend pass had been OK'd.

The nurse accepted her word and said, "OK, you know where your room is."

I told Helen I would see her within the week. I left furious and more distrustful of the "system" than my activist journeymen. At home, my mother said she had no knowledge of Helen's discharge. I could hardly wait to discuss this with my team leader the next morning.

He made numerous phone calls, which put responsibility on my mother, who insisted she had not received any correspondence from the hospital. However, there was no question that Helen was not ready for independent living. The questions were about where she should live and what supports were in order.

Dr. B. offered to do some family therapy if I would gather the members. All were more than willing, so, after two productive, satisfying sessions, Helen came home with the condition that she would be assigned to Team C (Albany City Unit). Dr. Press and Carole D., RN, attended community meetings and Activities of Daily Living (ADL) and other activities at her discretion. Within two weeks, she was settled into her own apartment, and, as she said, "Being like I'm supposed to be."

I never investigated the issue any further because school, Elaine, and health center community issues were all part of my eighteen-hour day. I remember joyfully putting it all behind me as I had dinner with John at the revolving restaurant in New York City and dancing our version of the tango before returning home in time for a class at eleven in the morning.

On October 21, Mom was rushed to Albany Medical Center Hospital for a broken hipbone from a fall down the stairs. Helen, visiting that day, found her and later got me at school. Now I could hardly wait for graduation. I felt overwhelmed with three or four meetings a week and on some weekends with health-center developers Dr. Birk; Dale Morgan; NAC board president, Dorothy Paul; and other staff from the medical college as well as working with the Urban League and Sister Maryellen Harmon to get the alternative school underway. I recommended Bob Peterson as principal. I had met and worked with him at Albany's Home for Children.

My appointment book documents the hours spent between SUNY, CDPC, community organization, and family, as well as the new learning and participatory experience of working with the League of Women Voters, learning the work and responsibilities of an independent school board and the process of separating the school board from Albany city government. When did I sleep? Thank God for Helen. I cooked and baked on the weekends, Helen was nurse, George and Howard were errand boys and visitors, and cousin Ella visited with special goodies.

As graduations approached, we all were in our own crisis of, "What's next?"

While on spring break, Elaine and her friends were home, and her father came to the house. My ability to watch their interaction while controlling myself from bursting this happy balloon was a tribute to my professional maturity. Subsequent Christmas cards from Bill were signed, "To the best friend I ever had—love."

It was graduation party time, I went down to old Westbury to see and hear Elaine speak, and then came back home for a backyard family celebration for the two of us. Then there was a night party for all of us—the four Hudson Valley recruits, Helen, Clara, Joyce, and SUNY grad Janice, and friends. All of my Link sisters were there, plus friends of the graduates. What an eventful night. Everyone wanted a picture with the graduates.

By June 1, I was back to full-time work at CDPC. All intakes were referred by Whitney Young Health Centers, having been named and dedicated in late '71 with a full cadre of professional and midlevel professionals on board. Within two months, the Urban League family-planning program in the south end of Albany was absorbed by Whitney Young. I had trained these outreach workers with my friend Dorothy. She accepted an RN position, and Mary Spriggs, MSW, took leave from Hudson River State Hospital to be a full-time mental-health worker. I felt complete, powerful, and accomplished.

We, as friends have been as close as sisters. We have been to Spain, North Africa, Egypt, Mexico, and Cartagena and, for twenty-four plus years, we escaped the frost of winters in Barbados.

Margaret Teabout, a Cobleskill graduate nutritionist pulled from Albany County Health Department by Dr. Kirk was in charge of setting up this program. I was asked to work with her as she set up a training program.

In July of '72 I took the ACSW exam and began thinking about private practice. I could reduce so much of my volunteering, and my retirement income could be supplemented by private work, which would also supplement Elaine's tuition at Amherst for her graduate degree.

Back at CDPC in the summer '72, I was acquainted with new staff and took on expanded responsibilities, as I seemed to be the most cognizant of our need to work toward being physically present in the community—"walk the talk."

Negotiations with Arbor Hill's Community Center opened Friday evenings for an Adolescent Social Time. for my cases and any other staff with teens who needed social skills, dancing, and so on. A weekly meeting with a facility field liaison and students from the school's group and community concepts course sat in on my "mothers" group. The word was getting around about how to call CDPC for help, and, as a result, Sara and I developed a training program for Albany County DSS workers.

We received many notes of thanks from individuals, businesses, and organizations for meetings to discuss our mutual responsibilities for the deinstitutionalized persons and the how, when, where, and why of their needs to refer persons for help.

I was called to the main office of mental hygiene to listen to community complaints about our adolescent program at Ten Broeck Street. I should not have been surprised, since seven to ten days earlier, I had a meeting with a parent who expressed concerns about her son's behavior after attending the day program.

Main office staff, several community people, and adolescent program staff welcomed me in the huge conference room. The program staff brought complaints about the director and the various therapeutic-learning techniques and games that were played. As a result of this meeting, the program eventually closed, and I was later asked to work with an OMRDD staff to develop a different program model for adolescents.

I resigned as chair of the personnel committee of CDPC with gratitude and understanding from Dr. Kraft. I declined an invitation to join the New York State Mental Health Association, feeling the need to keep my volunteer energy focused with the current organization and developing groups, speaking and participating in several church programs, several meetings at Danemora with the "Phase-out Reentry" group whose expectations relative to home in eighteen months needed to be explored. Through the community "Parents Against Drugs" program, this connection was made.

The local Black Social Workers (now National Association of Black Social Workers) were approached by our Haitian psychiatrist Dr. Celeston and his wife to conference in Haiti to explore the issue of transracial adoption of children and adolescents. Days of planning, fund-raising, and subject presentations took place from October '72 until February 24. We were welcomed by the minister of Haiti and treated as royalty. Social workers from all over the state came to fill our bus to New York and support our presentations. One attendee had a birthday on March 1, so a jazz party was held for her. I met with Dr. Duyong and his family. He was director of the mental hospital in Haiti. His wife and four girls were so gracious. The prime minister and the US ambassador to Haiti invited us to her home.

During the fall of '72, while I was planning the social-work event, Elaine informed me of her own event, due in April '73. She left school and came home to plan for her new role and responsibility "definitely without a husband." What could we—her mother and grandmother—say? "Think about how you have felt with and without your father?"

So, the fall of '72 and winter of '73, were mentally, physically, and emotionally draining. My parents having court appearances before Judge Keegan opened another valuable contact. He was respectful, honoring my position and asking relevant questions about the patient and treatment plans, followed by a lecture to the client. On several occasions over the years, he offered quick, pertinent advice on a personal family matter.

By March, the administrators at CDPC and ERDS (Eleanor Roosevelt Developmental Services) agreed that I would be the most likely person to implement a program for educable retarded and mentally ill adolescents. Dr. Hugh LaFave and his staff worked from a storefront location on lower Madison Avenue, while Dr. Alan Kraft (CDPC director) was in the process of moving from the mental-hygiene building on Holland Avenue to the ancient girls' academy structure opposite Washington Park. Both programs awaited the completion of permanent facilities. I met with their program staff, discussing the need to share skills between mental-health aides and teachers.

I interviewed a young man referred by Whitney Young Health Center who had been working with teens in a recently closed program. I was so excited to have him in the program. I immediately discussed his being hired with the personnel director. He questioned whether I should wait until someone from ERDS could interview him as well. I was negotiating my upgrade in terms of the adolescent program and CDPC career ladder.

At home, we were supporting Elaine with her plans for the baby. Debbie had eventually left Charlton School to live with her aunt in Watervliet. She graduated high school and went to Philadelphia to visit or live with her mother and eight siblings. On April 23, 1973, I was off to the hospital with Elaine, and on April 24, my grandson was born. His father, Peter Harper, came. It was my first meeting with him. I knew I didn't give a very warm welcome, but my goal was to have him with Elaine, name the baby boy, and sign his birth certificate. They named him Onaje Senka Harper, the sensitive leader of his people.

When we came home, Helen was more excited than Mom and me. Relatives were in and out. On one especially warm day, I took Onaje to the backyard to get the sun and hold him up for blessings. Janice's son, Jamal, who was eighteen months older, was also with us. For the next three or four years, they were like brothers.

Mom, Helen, and I couldn't seem to get enough of this boy. Howard and George were also fascinated by him. I became more focused on what the next five years before retirement would be like with Onaje in the picture.

I received a call from a woman who was in need of someone to talk to. She had called the main office and was given my number, which was interesting. I saw her several times in the cafeteria at 44 Holland Avenue—by that time, our program had moved to Madison Avenue. Larry Burwell, director of Urban League, offered his conference room any time after five thirty. So many doors were opening.

I met with Pete Jones at the League for support and to give him practical subjects for his idea for starting a health career program. He opened on North Pearl Street. The program was successful, and Urban League expanded it and took over, midsummer. I had closed or transferred my cases and started meeting with Dr. Dave Gottesmen and teacher Elaine Flagg from ERDS.

By September, I had completed the write-up for the adolescent program, and, on September 5, presented the "Room 181 Adolescent Program" to the CDPC unit chiefs. As adolescents were referred to the Room-181 program, our staff from CDPC and ERDS was supplemented by volunteer students from the community-services unit of SUNY, and part-time psychiatrists Zori K. and Arlene R. D., who worked directly with me and the staff.

The school district, court social services programs, and churches responded to my request for a community advisory board. The dissatisfaction of the program came from the Milne School building occupants, so after the first year, our program relocated to a Lark Street facility that was later vacated by the medical-college health-center planning team.

Our program grew and continued extraordinary working relationships through the daily teaching, exploring therapeutic sessions, and home visits—weekly multiple family therapy sessions that followed dinner.

It wasn't until the middle of '74 that I was informed of the tension between CDPC and ERDS. It seemed that ERDS would take over the program and my "item." I (and Bill) would become ERDS staff. My response, echoed by Bill, was, "Thanks, but no thanks." With four years to retirement, I wanted no more challenges in terms of different staff ideologies as their organization was in the process of reorganizing. The adolescents in the program were evaluated, assessed, and referred to the appropriate programs when they could accommodate them. Family visits continued by each staff in the home or facility in which a teen was temporarily placed.

The one and one-half years I administrated this program spread my name throughout the upstate area. Kingston Children's Home requested that I consider working with them on a case-to-case basis. United Black Parents brought Dr. Ken Clark Senior, and Maureen Joyce asked for a session with adolescent parents in her maternity program. I was recommended to attend an R. K. Rice Institute group relation in a hospital setting in New York City. I felt as if I had been through this for the past five or six years.

However, in April '74, a Las Vegas, San Francisco, and California cost vacation helped wash the "hospital" out of my world. As we returned to CDPC, our new Albany city unit director, Tom Tunney, asked for a complete review of my work from '69 to the present. I also learned that plans for the new building would not include "overnight" for adolescents, so what area would they need, since there would definitely be a community of eighteen- to twenty-one-year olds.

I began to schedule my late afternoons and evenings around when I had to pick up Onaje, and when the center needed me to interview or train staff.

I was organizing a community task force for the Albany city unit, similar to my adolescent-program model, maintaining a caseload of twenty, plus being the team leader of six unit personnel. I felt overwhelmed but confident that I could—and did—handle it.

As our team met to discuss how, where, and who in our area needed what and our best way to approach serving the needs, we began the model for community mental-health programs. Joyce recommended a landlord-and-tenants meeting. Jim recognized the growing alcoholism among seniors in the various housing developments. Bill continued with adolescents and supported Terry in considering courts and jail projects. Ironically I had received a call from Catholic diocese asking for consultation at the social services office of Cathedral. Following several visits to address the problems, Helen became the team liaison for that particular site.

Jim and Clara

Our next challenge was to conduct workshops during the CDPC open house at the official opening of the hospital. Since our main focus was out, we highlighted the positive areas in the building that were community friendly: the two theaters, conference rooms, schoolrooms, and so forth. As a result of our open house, I was asked to accompany another CDPC social worker to develop a three-month training session for Albany County Department of Social

Services. After that, Sara W. and I took a week's vacation in Fort Lauderdale, Florida.

The calls came in from various agencies, which prompted the unit chief to ask me to head up a community task force. An answer to the community's call— a community contacts task force. We held monthly meetings to exchange who everyone was, what they did, and how can we could help the client. I insisted that we include grocers, landlords, and neighbors as well. These are the people who really service our clients twenty-four hours a day, seven days a week. This monthly meeting of community and county agency representatives as well as churches and dioceses became the strength and voice of mental health.

A note from the CDPC administrator acknowledged the success of the positive working relationship between our state program and the county mental-health agency. I personally understood and could attest to the frustration of seven years.

One evening before returning home, I didn't feel well, so I had my blood pressure checked at Whitney Young Health Center. The nurse practitioners were alarmed; they called my doctor, requesting that he stand by or recommend hospitalization. He prescribed medication and set up an appointment for the next day.

This was a real wake-up call for me. I would definitely retirement in August '78 when I would be fifty-five. Every weekend would be a meaningful relaxed time with the family, and vacations would not be associated with career, organization building, or better New York State program development—Spain, North Africa, Morocco, Senegal, and Cartagena. I knew and understood Elaine's commitment to improving the various jobs she took, from teaching to enhancing the health-careers program at Arbor Hill Community Center and state government while completing her master's in education from St. Rose and raising her baby boy, Onaje.

Emily married and was raising two girls and a boy same age as Onaje. Debbie was working for a Watervliet pharmacy before taking off to Florida, and then settling in New Haven, Connecticut, with a friend whose two-year old Debbie immediately "mothered appropriately." This seemed to be quite acceptable to the mother, Pam, for a short time. Then after my trip to Mexico in '76, I got a call from Deb, who wanted to come home, work and, eventually continue school. After reviewing house rules and school expenses, she came home.

A summer weekend brought two of mom's siblings from Huntington to visit, proving that "the road does run both ways." What a celebration with an older sister Floss and the youngest brother, Toby (Howard).

By the fall of '76, I was involved in more personal family issues, which called for decision-making that would have long-term consequences. My monthly doctors' visits and high blood-pressure medications were further incentives to plan for a retirement that would provide fun time with individual family members and friends, funds to supplement my retirement until social security would be available, and free time to travel when or wherever.

My concentration now was on continuing to build and expand the work of Albany City Unit (Team C) by documenting the western movement of our clients; setting up a part-time satellite office at the vacant CYO building on upper Second Street; and accepting a visiting psychologist Manuela Z. from Germany to shadow me as I replaced Helen at the Albany Dioceses social work office, because she now served their weekly client needs up in Berne-Know. I continued weekly meetings with Parents Against Drugs (PAD) and conducted monthly group meetings with Ed C. at Comstock Prison. The men in the group were being discharged in eighteen to twenty-four months and accepted the need to discuss the realities of family, home, and community life after any number of years away.

As the Albany City Unit expanded its community contacts and as the staff of CDPC became more hospitalized, more licensed clinical psychologists were brought on board, and several graduate degree nurses with bachelor of arts and sciences degrees and interns. I became team leader of one of four Albany County teams comprising of two Hudson Valley human-services graduates, two male social workers, one male nurse, one female nurse, and a BA psychologist transfer from the Latham team. There were several off-site meetings to acquaint, mix, and understand that we served a necessary purpose.

Human Services Grads

During the next few years, the graduate psychologist expressed her dissatisfaction with being on this team; however, resigning was not an option for her at this time. She was recently married and her husband was financing undergraduate school with part-time job. I recognized her multiple issues, including absenteeism, and that she conversed only with other CDPC staff psychologists. After identifying and acknowledging her intake skills, I assigned this team task to her. The process then involved sharing with me assignment with the team psychiatrist, developing a treatment plan including family and community contacts, patient groups meetings, and team meeting presentations and feedback.

One day she came in with a black glove on one hand saying that it was treatment for an old Olympic skating injury. I excused her from all duties and suggested she go home. The charge on her record was "sick leave." I told her to think hard about her position, attitude, and why she had been transferred. Upon her return, she became a model team member. She was supportive, congenial, and willing to trade or substitute on-call weekend duty.

I remembered similar experiences working as a supervisor in taxation and finance. There would be one or more instances of insubordination, prompted by jealousy, racism, gender, or whatever at every level.

My practice facility teacher had identified and labeled my ability to recognize and deal with these issues as "intuition." *Whatever.*

As the center geared up toward a community open house at the hospital, I spent more time with the agencies. I refused any responsible board or staff position but enjoyed discussions about program improvement, such as Urban League starting a guild, Council of Community Services, Society of Friends, and Legal Aid. I did accept a three-day trip to Washington, where I met with a diverse group to discuss and suggest new directions. From a Hawaiian, I learned of their history and her own anger and need to become a legal-aid advocate and hopefully a board member to help the families who had been displaced by the wealthy planters.

I returned to the ACU team excited about the open house while I focused on the proposal for a program at 340 Second Street, identifying other staff, perhaps interns and half-time persons, who might be involved. This "next step" program would include, in addition to case-advisory appointments, home visits and Friday evening and Saturday morning time for neighborhood police-unit issues.

Approval for the program budget and the hiring of a part-time MSW schoolmate made me consider my retirement. I resigned as chair of affirmative action. I transferred the follow-up of "the need for a Spanish-speaking staff" to an initiative for a community advisory board to CDPC.

The community contacts task force was a three-year, demonstrated interest group comprised of spokesmen from the nine-county human-services community as a supportive. It seemed to me that it had made such a significant impact that it would be a natural process for CDPC to accept it. The newly hired public-relations person, Marge LeBrun, attended our task force meeting and agreed with me. Again I was reminded of my tax-and-finance issue when the commissioner wasn't ready to deal with the cultural diversity in the state and the implications for civil service hiring and training.

The June 28, 1977, open house from twelve to four involved lunch, facility tours, and workshops. Dr. Kraft greeted the attendees in the large auditorium.

Many positive responses were received, and one in particular was directed to the ACUCC task force and me from the board of visitors. As the clients became accustomed to the facility, we noticed that their most comfortable area was the cafeteria. The staff tried hard to engage them in Ping-Pong and table games, but, in most cases, it became staff versus staff. I had been given a highly prized second-floor corner office overlooking Myrtle and South Lake Avenues.

The south wing was for inpatient bedrooms. Between my office and the hospital were the city unit secretary and offices of the psychiatrists. The third floor consisted of administrative offices and school and conference rooms.

Because my satellite-office proposal, "Next Step," had been accepted, I had to be more conscious of my work time and place, and particularly my time. Any unused vacation time over twenty hours was sacrificed, as opposed to sick time, which had no limits on accumulation. As a result, a birthday trip to Disney World for five-year-old Onaje was the most effective way of putting work issues in perspective.

Once back at work, I started scheduling staff hours, programs, and client services at the satellite office, as well as at home-base CDPC. I also scheduled a weekly evening group for "colored girls" as my major focus to provide a safe, supportive time and place to explore self-esteem and interpersonal and ethnic relationships—both male and female—child-rearing single parenthood, individual freedom, problem-solving, and goal planning. Bernadette was the anchor at the satellite office, with team members meeting area clients and my Friday evening and Saturday morning hours fulfilling the objectives of the program.

Vivian, jointly with Bill B., accepted more and more team responsibilities. By the spring of '78, the various neighborhood leaders were requesting more specific information about ACU and CDPC via the members of the advisory board. I felt satisfied with the work I had performed at CDPC, demonstrating the knowledge and skills of an older social worker. This was evidenced by the readiness of team members to work with me until my position was filled because, by this time, I was completely, unmistakably, and without a doubt retiring. The final blow was a notice that staff must return to the center. When I asked what happened to our commitment, I was told, "We have beds here to fill. You may stay out there, but others must be here."

The meeting with the team was most difficult. I had to explain that our successful community mental-health approach was costing the state X number of dollars because the bedrooms were not being used. Albany Medical Center had closed one of its psychiatric units, so our nine-county area had, indeed, set a workable pattern of mental-health client advocacy. The problem seemed to be hospital-oriented, career medical professionals who were reluctant to accept the total package of client and community outside of the hospital building.

I had many visits from staff to my CDPC corner office, asking, "Are you really leaving?" I had to ask Dr. Kraft to call a general staff meeting. Marge settled the issue when she interviewed me for the August issue of the *State Mental Hygiene News*.

I was surprised to learn that our administrator, Dr. Kraft, was also leaving. The interview was lengthy. I appreciated her sensitive comment about my work. "Continue to make real the commitment to community care," she said.

I became a community member of the advisory board while Eileen Cregg cochaired with Tom Murphy and John Corrado. Meanwhile, Marge Leburn represented CDPS administration.

Joyce Russo and Helen Hopkins planned a retirement party for me, inviting special help from organizations, community, friends, and family. What an overwhelming affair at the Desmond in August '78. John asked, "Are you finished now?"

My response was, "With what?"

Desmond Americana

My community and family affairs over the past two years had been so challenging and, at times, nearly spirit breaking that the CDPC work was a break.

Debbie and Pam's difficulties were compounded by their drug involvement
plus control over the child. Elaine's apartment was more than adequate, except
the landlord ignored the roof that needed repair. Since he and his family occupied the ground floor of this beautiful two-family home, one rain-stained ceiling
and kitchen wall didn't bother him. She finally moved to State Street, within
walking distance of her job at the Capitol. As Onaje made himself known in the
Winthrop Avenue neighborhoods. I looked forward to birthday parties, games,
holidays, and anytime playtime. Dad went from the VA hospital to Eden Nursing
Home, and then back to VA when he developed pneumonia. He died in January
'78.

Howard and George displayed awesome support and leadership. They helped
Mom, Helen, and Onaje through the process of the funeral and the drive from
Albany to Long Island Military Cemetery, and then back home. The next several
months brought further mourning, as, in all large families, each passing left an
extra-heavy mourning process on the living. However, I managed to squeeze a
week in the Virgin Islands at the request of my friend Dorothy. She was reluctant
to respond to her ill father's call until her husband reminded her of the responsibility she owed her children.

The numerous "vacations" were therapeutic. A special chapter will be de-
voted to each. As my calendar documented closing work activities, I noted planning for Elaine's party and doctor's appointments August 14 and 30. I had been
keeping bimonthly appointments since '76 and questioned the need to continue.
However, my doctor said, "I'll let you know."

Of course, the community work was not more stressful than the CDPC
arena. The Whitney Young Health Center establishment, board and staff organization, and program development, all called for local, district, and federal
review and acceptance.

I became board president for several years between Albany and New York,
and Washington was directed to Izetta Fisher (the board member representing
the Urban League) and Dorothy Paul (administrative assistant to the center directors and Dr. McBride). However, phone calls, immediate document signing,

and mediation were mine to deal with. Board-member disagreements kept me on my professional toes. My social time was special with Links, M. C. Laughtons, Urban League guild members, and family.

Albany District links

While in Chicago attending a "black family" conference, I connected with Cousin Bob and his daughter and granddaughter, whom I hadn't seen in over fifteen years. How relaxing and free to talk of old times—What if? Have you heard from...?—while eating and drinking to the future of our grandchildren.

Real joy comes not from
ease or riches or from the
praise of men, but from
doing something worthwhile.
—Anonymous

CHAPTER 8

PRIVATE PRACTICE: PUTTING IT ALL TOGETHER

I returned to wrap up, clear out, and prepare for the retirement party and private practice with Bernadette. For my birthday, Elaine gave me a beautifully carved wooden sign for the office window and phone calling cards in addition to the spectacular reception and dinner. What a launch into doing my own thing.

Now I set my own work schedule. Wow—freedom and control. First I had to match my income with my prior salary while expanding my vacations, select volunteer activities, and home time with family.

A mandate for jury duty on September 11 controlled my immediate schedule. It was a great new experience that provided the opportunity to meet up with several old acquaintances from Arbor Hill and to learn the court procedures beyond mental-health clients' first appearances.

I received a request from Catholic Family Service to train the volunteers in the Parent Aide Program two times a week, consider a position as consultant in a young woman's alternative jail program by injecting social-work values, and to write the goals and terminology into a grant being submitted for funding to the state. I received a request to join the Friends Society Group to develop a mediation-training program. The Hudson YWCA asked me to regulate a six- to nine-week women's group. The Kingston Children's Home wanted me to work with an Albany child and needed someone in Albany to work with the family plus meet with the Kingston staff monthly to share progress toward the goal of having the child return to a receptive DSW-accepted home. Each exposure was an in-depth learning experience, which influenced my practice, volunteer-organization outlook, and personal home life.

293 HUDSON AVE

When my original partner, Bernadette, opted out of our practice, I filed my résumé with the Federal Civil Service, getting a permanent social-work grade to use "just in case." Bernadette continued part time with CDPC until individual appointments totally covered office expenses. I leased the space on weekends to a friend to show her quilts and have customers pick up their food orders. I continued contact with CDPC, however, since my Community Agency Advisory Board monthly meetings were thriving under the community leadership of Eileen and John Carrado. Marge LeBurn (CDPC community liaison) attended periodically, as they asked for training similar to the continuing education program at SUNY, crisis intervention with people with mental illness.

All our days were full as my contact with the group was from nine to eleven one Saturday for three months and an orientation session for Albany Medical College Residents, "Blacks in America." By the end of '78, I had set my schedule—office hours, program consultation and supervision of staff, board membership, and organization monthly meetings. I was home every weekday by six and had no weekend commitments. I remember feeling exalted and in control for the first time since my first years in Albany.

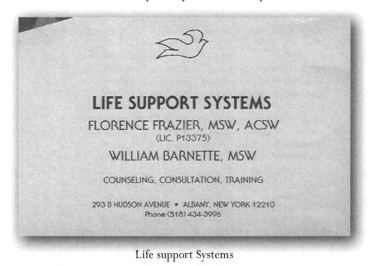

Life support Systems

Whitney Young Health Center director Dr. McBride and I, as board president, became a free-standing governing board of the community health center. This supported my decision to resign from the board when the Arbor Hill resident male members were clamoring for positions.

Before Onaje and I went to Disney World, we had many celebrations at home. So many Aquarians in the family. I relaxed and enjoyed Links and Lawton Club meetings, which were always held at members' homes. I accepted an Urban League guild membership, which included an enjoyable Saturday orientation and a legal-aid board membership that required a trip to Washington for a national training session of board members. For me, it was a vacation and learning time. I met several Hawaiians, who enlightened us all and shared in depth with me the deep prejudice and history of fraudulent land transactions that have now divided the islands into "them and us." Reporting back to Larry Klepper, director, and Jodie Holmes, receptionist, I felt that I really didn't want another "board experience" and felt badly about setting a one-year limit to my term.

I was seeing more couples in my practice, so I asked Bill Barnette to join me. As an MSW, perhaps he would continue on to grad school, except that he had twin boys, who were the same age as Onaje, to raise. Even in the seventies, two-working-parent families didn't find it easy to cover all needs. We conducted monthly parent meetings at The Boys Club and submitted articles to the *South End Scene* relative to resolving relationship, family, and community issues.

In the spring of 1980, the Urban League asked us to read and give our opinion of a recent grant from the Department of Labor, a summer educational career-oriented program focused on early high-school students, based on the "far-west model" in California. I found it to be a needed program, especially the vocation and career components. My only questions were who would be the morning educators, and what about their orientation and overall training?

The objective of the grant was to strengthen the students' basic math, English, reading, and speech skills and identify career goals that they would do an internship in the afternoon. I wrote an orientation and training program for staff that discussed the positive aspects of the program, which was accepted and proved to be such a success that it was funded for two years. It was then taken on by the school district to give credit to the participating students. What an exhilarating, fun, and productive summer.

At home for dinner with Onaje and Mom, I filled them in on the SAVE (Summer Adolescent Vocational Education) program. He asked if I knew what a TV announcer or weatherman had to learn. I took him to meet Bob K., who was very congenial. Bob walked him through the necessary education; gave him a tour of the facility, and explained the science of weather reporting from the central station to the local desk. To my surprise, as we were leaving, Bob K. bent to shake Onaje's hand. He expressed delight in his interest, and then said, "You'll probably be ready to take this job when I retire."

Onaje replied, "Oh no. I'm going to be an astronaut." Well, that was a real exit line.

Thinking back on this definitely stated goal, I recalled that Elaine had finished her grad work in education at St. Rose, and Debbie was ready to put behind the numerous issues that seemed to block her progress. She signed up at

Hudson Valley and was to enter the Arbor House Rehab Program. Educational goals were valued here.

We had a great family gathering at the bridal shower for Linda. A cousin came up from Long Island. It was her first venture away from Huntington. She was fifty years old, married, and the mother of eight. She cried until her brother-in-law took her back home at six in the morning. The other cousins stayed the weekend, getting to know their Albany cousins or the groom's family.

This September affair was only clouded for Elaine, Mom, and me by Deb being arrested. With the support of Arbor House staff, friends, and family, we carried on, and my visit to Albany County Jail was not welcome. Deb loudly rejected my suggestion for proper clothing for her court appearance, and I was told to go home.

So the holidays, family routine, board and club attendance, and work kept me sane. With Dot Bryan, I planned and spent ten days in Cartagena and Bogota, Colombia, and relaxed in the sun, sand, and sea while considering the request from Whitney Young's director, Osborn, for help in building up the psychiatric department.

I supervised the MSW and met with the psychiatrist weekly at Whitney Young while in the process of securing an Article 28 licensure under New York Health Department. The most difficult and frustrating aspect of this two-year endeavor was the disconnect between the records department, the social worker, and the psychiatrist. Since the agency was unable to secure an Article 28 standing, the funding for psychiatry was out. I continued with the social worker to develop a senior services network in various community housing facilities until the funding ceased.

My board work with the Council of Community Services increased as I met with Mayor Corning to discuss the goal of the council relative to supporting the needs of the community by utilizing the United Way's survey results. Joseph Cohen began the work but resigned from the board for personal reasons.

I reviewed my "other than work" schedule. I met with the dean and faculty of the School of Social Welfare about the position of part-time field instructor. I could see the value of students being a part of council's work as well as my developing more "community" field placements for all students.

So I walked through the door part time, having been cleared by the retirement system and the school's requirement to document its need for me each year. Of course, my numerous questions about the program, location, and courses brought me onto the "downtown campus" with Dean Kirk and faculty including John Oliver, the only black faculty member. My biggest issue was why was the social-work undergraduate field program was situated in the basement of the uptown campus when the classes and faculty were downtown. I made contact with Heidi McKinley, who directed the community volunteer program for the university. We often remarked about our "luxurious" accommodations.

I may not have had CDPC on my Rolodex, but they had my number. I got a call and a written request to review a patient-staff complaint and give my opinion after interviewing the parties involved, and then a referral to Williams College to discuss an interracial incident on campus to which Bill and I responded. After meeting with students and faculty, I was asked to join their counseling unit seeking student referrals or self requests. At that time, I had only one day free a week, which they accepted. In the fourth semester, I informed them of my inability to continue and that I would not be returning in the fall.

Mom had said she was fearful of being alone during the dark winter nights. I usually didn't get home those Monday evenings until well after six. Then we experienced a plane crash two blocks from our home. At this time, other than the Williams College work, my schedule of activities covered eight in the morning until five. Many committee meetings, pinochle group, and so forth were held at home after I cooked dinner and took it upstairs to Mom.

One night during supper upstairs, Mom said, "Who is going to care for you when you're like me?" I laughed and told her not to worry. I'd be lucky if I lived as long as she did.

Within a year, the dean assured me of an office downtown, from which I operated for five years. Again the new experience brought challenges that tested my strength, faith, and beliefs. I insisted upon weekly field seminars. How else would I get to know myself, others, and the community of placements? I established numerous new resources for interns. The most difficult one to convince was the Department of Corrections. While this was a part-time position, I was being recruited for several school committees, which I refused. However, the monthly facility meeting was required.

I experienced such fulfillment throughout the years from 1981 to 1996. The training, teaching, and workshops, as well as being in control of time and place was such a high.

In the midst of the new life experience, my support system shifted; strengthening in friendships and losing in family. The Huntington aunts and uncles were passing, which weighed heavily on Mom and forced me to tighten up my work schedule to combine vacations with trips to Long Island more often so that the remaining sisters and brothers could be together.

I enjoyed Atlantic City Boardwalk sand and sea with my sister-in-law Barbara and Senegal West Africa with Dorothy as her resident son David escorted us around the country. I could spend a week in the library searching ancestors.

John continued to get positions in any of the correctional or other state facilities with an opening for an engineer assistant. By the end of '82, he had an appointment at Warwick and purchased a house in Glens Falls, had joined a church in Saratoga, and the NAACP was his challenge. He traveled weekends from Orange County to Glens Falls, stopping along the way for dinner and urging me to participate in remodeling an ancient building. Been there, done that; thanks, but no thanks. I did however support his church and workshop sessions with the NAACP. But the nature of his past life was a caution for me. I had met his sister and was told of two brothers.

Ironically, while I was in Spain, I just missed seeing him. But John would not talk about his prior relationships and offspring, if any. By the end of '82, my friend Mary was expressing shared feelings of exhaustion, depression, and winter blues. We found a week's all-inclusive vacation to Barbados. It opened nother door. For the next two decades we refreshed and revived ourselves, and encouraged Dorothy, Barbara, and others to join us.

When Onaje was sixteen, he joined me for a week. This particular experience was like when I left home at nineteen and came to Albany. That first island vacation supported me through the most difficult year. In '83, Deb was sentenced, and Mom had a stroke and passed in June. Elaine, strong and decisive, stepped up and took charge. I was in a complete daze, following directions from funeral-home staff and gentle suggestions from Elaine's friend who was constantly by her side at the house. This was the second time in my life I broke down with uncontrollable tears on Leonard Harper's shoulder as they lowered Mom into the grave. Helen, George, and Howard grieved with me. Ella and others joined in remembering Ms. Clara. I visited Helen more often as she was around the block from my office and didn't like coming to Winthrop Avenue. Her chosen neighborhood was downtown. We all restructured our lives and relationships with each other. It was a new life, calling for serious introspection.

Thanks to Onaje I knew the names of my neighbors within the square block and felt quite safe and connected. However, I had little time to even think about being alone as work, school, Club, acceptance on the Black Arts and Cultural Committee, and an opportunity to see cousin Bob and family in Chicago as I attended the Urban League Family Conference kept me busy.

From this occasion, I brought back tapes describing the Black Child Development Institute. Its mission and goals were so relevant to our needs that I shared them with Linda, the principal of Arbor Hill School). She spread the word and an Albany affiliate was established.

Did I refuse any request at this time? Oh, yes. After one term on the Next Step board, I excused myself. National Coalition of 100 Black Women? No thanks. It was a repeat of other nationally affiliated clubs. And, again, I refused with-honor invitations to Greek Letter organizations. I spent more time with my older friend Helen, as she, too, was adjusting to late-life physical problems and losses. Cousin Ella was also facing possible serious health issues and child and grandchild losses as well as needing to move.

As we were both on the board of the New Arbor Hill Community Center, Inc., Ella looked forward to being able to continue. However, while she was in the hospital, I heard of a lovely house in Menands that was being sold by an acquaintance. I passed along the information, and, as a result, her grandchildren made all the arrangements for the move. She, wrapped in blankets, hospital gown, and slippers, directed the movers as they plowed through the spring slush and placed furniture. This split-level house was perfect as her daughter and grandson could live in the basement apartment.

The good time in Barbados was followed by the trip to Old Westbury as Elaine received the Honorable Alumni's Award, a positive reception from Debbie when her aunt and I visited, and the lovely luncheon and huge African mask I was given as I left DSW. DSW had an abundance of field placements, more than enough for both BS and MSW students, and two field supervisors were no longer needed. So I was free again.

Another door flew open when the director of the New York State Board for Social Welfare needed a part-time LCSW-R to review applications for licensure. Since I had moved my private practice to my residence, I worked from the State office for several months to become oriented to the various licensure procedures. I later worked from home, picking up and delivering the applications and kept accurate logs of the time I spent reviewing them.

Two planned island vacations supported my gradual increase in work—St. Ann's, County Department of Social Services, consulting with Carver Health, writing a social-service program for Arbor Hill Center while going through staff changes at Arbor House. Mary, Dorothy, and I loved Jamaica, and, had it not been for Dorothy's purse being stolen during the night, we might have considered it as our yearly vacation spot.

Back at a seniors' meeting at Arbor Hill during game time, I said, "No more smoking for me." I smoked my last cigarette in September 1986. With my game partners, smoking held no temptation.

While coming, going, and attending our Smith family reunion at Heckshire Park, Islip, I learned and taught so much. What a gathering! Most didn't know Jacksons and Fraziers were at a Smith family reunion. However, by the time the stories were told, pictures, shown and side-by-side encounters took place, the "tree" was overburdened with branches. One young cousin, Shawna, had recently been accepted at Memorial Hospital School for Nurses in Albany, but, despite her mother's urging, she didn't think she could go so far from home and wondered if they had a dormitory.

Needless to say, Shawna came to live with me for two semesters, and then missed her friend George and got married. Her mother said, "Well, since you don't want school, I do," and she signed her own application for nurses-aide training at a school in Farmingdale.

As recommended by my primary doctor, I visited a cardiologist before getting on the road south with Mary. I got the all cleared and had no serious withdrawal from smoking symptoms. We were off to Atlanta, Georgia to visit the Martin Luther King church and memorial and various restaurants where meetings had been held. During our stay, Atlanta had snow. The hostesses announced, "There are warm biscuits in the oven and coffee. Help yourselves. We got to go home." As several other guests with us stood wide-eyed and open-mouthed, the staff left.

I returned home to check on work, family, and friends, and then set off to Barbados. More and more, I saw myself actually alive and living while I was there. This feeling manifested in my being at the top of my professional work; being of practical support to family; and driving Onaje (after his junior-high graduation) to Croton, and then on to Bedford Hills to visit Deb, and then to Long Island for the funeral of my father's sister Aunt Bess.

By the fall, I became aware of tension at Carver Health Center as their service provisions and policies challenged the historic institutions. Establishing a structured social-service unit and engaging more of the Schenectady community pushed all Carver staff to function at their best levels. With Director Izetta, we developed the social-services unit and assigned work and titles according to need, task, and title. As referrals came from medical staff and walk-in clients, the entire staff needed to dialogue, understand, and share the goals of each client seeking service. There were three MSW students, one BSW permanent employee, and a community service worker under my supervision.

The receptionist was immediately onboard and understood the concept of the service-process needs of the client. The field coordinator for the Graduate School of Social Welfare approved the program as appropriate for students and understood my role as consultant, my hours, and the expectations of the school. By the holidays, we were all settled, and I looked forward to Barbados. Private-practice cases transferred to appropriate services and MSW classmate

Bernadette was willing to help out at the health center if necessary. How thankful I was to have the physical and spiritual recharge to look back on upon my return.

Izetta had been replaced by Walter Isaacs as director of the health center. No discussions or plans had been made for a good-bye or thank you party by either the board or staff. My three-hour meeting with the new director led to more positive action for the social-work department and relocation from the basement to the second floor.

Bernadette accepted full-time employment given the center professional units throughout; more training for the community workers and receptionists; and orientation, knowledge and understanding of individuals and institutions in the tri-city that interfaced with the health center.

At a meeting with Izetta, we talked about doors opening when others seemed to slam shut. She was quite enthusiastic about being home to entertain family and friends, garden, and used her pool and knowing that her husband would be overjoyed with her being at home. I, too, used my time at home to oversee the installation of new windows throughout the house; replant a garden; and motored to Martha's Vineyard, New Hampshire, to accept a distinguished alumni award from Rockefeller College School of social welfare.

I was, once again, compelled to respond to a request for support. Evelyn Williams, the new director of Whitney Young Community Health Center, discussed the need for outreach training for employees in several programs. Her background as a social worker and director of a large community-based mental-health facility in New York City humbled me.

In addition, she hired a young MSW to head the drug program. Could I find time to supervise her? I shared my current schedule with her, including my priority, which was Izetta's party.

A Black Child Development Conference in Washington was a pleasure from the start—planning with Bill and Betty (as director of Arbor Hill, she needed to be there), stopping along the way to pick up Mary Spriggs in Poughkeepsie, but primarily making sure that the young male program director attended. Listening to problems being solved and discussions of pros and cons, my cup runneth over!

Upon our return, the Arbor Hill board was pleased to hear the positive report from the directors.

As the year came to a close, we planned a real Thanksgiving at home with immediate family, friends, and two foreign students. What fun! Of course, by the time I left for Barbados in January, there were reciprocal gatherings. In March, the jury-duty summons was for a grand jury—a new experience. I can't help but think that my responses had some effect on my not ever being called again for jury duty. A fiftieth reunion plus a family wedding took me back home. Both affairs highlighted that "the times, they are a-changin'."

At the reunion, as during our school years, I was the only black person. A male classmate said, "We wanted to learn the dance that you were doing. [The jitterbug.] We saw you in the gym with the guys and at the theater."

The wedding was interracial. On the way back home, I stopped to see Debbie and, again, felt guilty about having exposed her to such a world.

And then another door opened. Unreal! Izetta had been hired as director of Carver Community Center, which provided a professionally staffed day care and recreation facility. She had the possibility of securing funds for a foster-care prevention program and needed "social-work philosophy and jargon" to complete her proposal.

Several meetings at Carver and in my home seemed to be satisfactory. Meantime, I had been annoyed by periodic pain in my mouth since summer that I diagnosed as "tongue bites from nerves." I was referred to an ear, nose, and throat specialist (ENT), who sent me for a biopsy. Judy was with me when the news was given to me, "Cancer. Return to your ENT surgeon." That was November 28, 1990.

Dr. Paonessa described his procedure to Elaine and me. He said, "Yes, I will remove part of the tongue and slit the throat to assure I've removed surrounding possible damage." He and Elaine talked further, but I was in a daze.

From his office, I went to St. Peter's Hospital. I awoke in the recovery room answering questions. "Who are you? Where did you come from?" The doctor later explained that while I was sedated, prior to surgery, I talked nonstop, calling out names and places that were unfamiliar to anyone in the operating room. He explained what the next days, weeks, and months would be like and answered my main questions. "How did this happen?" He said that research verified cigarettes and alcohol.

With family and friends standing by me and Izetta, Isaac, and Bernadette's assurance, "We need you on the job," recuperation in December and January was a story in itself. I had daily visits from my neighbor friend, Onaje, sister Helen, brothers Howard and George, and nieces dropping by. I completed many puzzles, which I subsequently had framed. The three-dimensional ones were challenging but were so beautiful when completed that I had to take photos of them.

Izetta's program was funded. She came to discuss the selections of a program director and possible BS and MSW students. By mid-January, I was able to come off my liquid, soft diet but was warned, "No fish, unless it's filet." I could not (and still cannot) detect bones. Every six months for two years, I saw the doctor until I was transferred for follow-up to the Oncology-Hematology Group, from which I was cleared and discharged in 2002. It was so good to be on the road again and in control of my own comings and goings.

I had a contract with the Foster Care Prevention Program at Carver two times a week, a close-out from Carver Health Center, and attendance at the BSW and conference in Atlanta. I was overjoyed by the motor trip home via Raleigh-Durham, North Carolina, and, best of all, Gettysburg. I couldn't thank Janice and Eddie enough for the drive through a part of the country as historical as the Hudson. I was back in time to receive my Tribute to Women award from the YWCA.

As a board member, I held racism workshops and held several committee responsibilities. I became overwhelmed when Urban League also presented an award for my volunteer work with the guild and a wide range of community programs. I humbly accepted these awards and promptly swallowed the frustration and anxiety it provoked. I would question why me. Others were also volunteering out there. John said, "It's the way you go about it, with a smile and no nonsense."

Burwell said, "Tell me who else? Who?"

I said, "Dot Bryan."

He said, "She's not happy with it or with herself."

I missed having Mom to help with this, so the next Sunday, I visited Ella. She said, "You should be getting paid for all the time you put in for the club and organizations. I'm glad that I'm not on the Arbor Hill Community Center board anymore. Everybody has a different opinion, and I think they just want time away from home, kids, or husbands!"

Needless to say, this wasn't helpful to me—so I kept on smiling and accepted membership in Center for Women in Government.

I wasn't particularly interested in this university's implementation of the governor's Liberty Partnership program. Onaje, as the senior class president, and other national scholarship winners and Mrs. Cumo with several students were pictured in a *Times Union* story about the program. The Center for Women in Government was community-focused.

Wow! How proud I was to find myself again in the palace at graduation where one of mine was center stage. This time Onaje, as class president, gave the keynote speech in which he honored Elaine, his mother, for his accomplishments. Then we said good-bye as he went off to Buffalo College.

I accepted a request from Mr. Jones (a project review on the adoption/foster-parenting program) funded by the New York State Department of Social Services that was being operated from a church in Schenectady. It was busy work! Then I had questioned why I was maintaining this huge house when it could be shared. The mortgage had long since been settled, and when I wanted any remolding, I applied for and received a loan for the amount. Before leaving, Onaje had worked with a contractor to restructure the back porch. That fall, I painted and carpeted.

I had work in Schenectady and Albany to work; duties to fulfill as an officer or committee person in my five organizations; obligations to family, Ella, Helen, Howard, George, and their children and grandchildren. I fled away to Barbados but returned to a difficult year of family illness and took care of them. "Just get over the need to social work!" I always acknowledged this positive work with Helen, so I closed off the issue of her mental state and set a time for weekly visits for doctors' appointments. At Helen's new apartment, neighbors and surroundings presented some anxious times for her. We made frequent visits to cousin Ella, as her oldest daughter was released from the hospital and subsequently died at her mother's home. Helen began to refuse to go for clinic or doctor's appointments.

She allowed the aide to shop and help with laundry, but when x-ray or other procedures were scheduled, she canceled or ignored them. She accepted the Meals on Wheels, but looked forward to our going out and still refused to consider living with me or any other family member.

By mid-June—three months home and her family illness and its consequences to consider, Ella's daughter living in the basement apartment was hospitalized.

Then the call from the coroner's office came to meet with George and Howard and make arrangements for Helen. She had been found deceased and identified by George, whose phone number was listed first in her book. I remember saying to myself, "She had this in mind all along—from the time she had to move—refusing her medical appointments. She knew that she was in control, and enough was enough." We welcomed and accepted the support of other family members and friends. If there was ever a time to be thankful for work (meetings, phone calls, and requests for ideas), and then alone time (meditation, prayer, and contemplation), it was now.

I accepted more workshop requests and short-term cases from wherever— even a bat waking me from a deep sleep, not once, but enough times that I called Howard and George, and we cornered it. That led to having an inspection of the chimney and attic.

I filled every hour, especially on the weekends—driving to Saratoga, Glens Falls, to assure John that we were indeed soul mates, but not a daily, living-together couple. He seemed to be as relieved as I. We continued dating on and off, exchanging books, and so forth. Further driving took me on the road to see Mary in Wappinger's Falls, and then Long Island.

Before my sixty-ninth birthday, I knew what constituted a "good life" for me. I paid the YMCA in order to use the warm pool two times a week. Although it didn't provide the salt and waves from the tide, it kept my body moving and provided time to meditate while floating on my back.

Wendy, who had come to Brooklyn from Barbados to visit relatives, took in the views of the Hudson to find me. Dorothy and I enjoyed sight-seeing with her, and we took a motor trip to Kingston to meet Mary via Amtrak. Wendy returned to Brooklyn, and we looked forward to seeing her in January.

My semiannual checkup result provoked some anxiety, as I was referred for a CT scan and to a cardiovascular specialist at St. Vincent's Hospital in New York. The results were gratifying. I was told to have a cardiology checkup yearly and my primary every three to six months.

I remember Thanksgiving at Elaine's with Onaje and Howard. What a feast, and a time to give thanks, as we had again just celebrated the release from pain of Ella's daughter. Since there were several adult males, perhaps one of them or the granddaughter Sue would take the apartment and be Ella's "caretaker."

I shared my travel plans at dinner—Egypt, and then Barbados. The response was unexpected, as Elaine was totally against Egypt, and I had questioning support from Howard. In his quiet way, he said, "They're pretty vocal about being anti-Westerners." I felt positive in assuring them about Elderhostel, an educational tour company out of Boston. I'd be going with Dorothy, her cousin Caroline from Long Island, and Mary. To think, I would be in the country that had fascinated me in fourth and fifth grades. I had recently clipped an article from *Time* or *Newsweek* about recent finds in the Sudan that predated Egypt's pyramids.

By the first week of January, I had covered all my work responsibilities, attended December meetings of all organizations, and let all and SUNY know that I couldn't be available until March 6.

I kept a daily record of Egypt with multiple pictures. We were housed in a motel on the palace grounds and toured the magnificent structure. The pool was available to us, and we were encouraged to pack bathing suits, but, as luck would have it, the coldest January was recorded, and Dorothy thanked Mary for a sweater coat.

In Albany, when we were boarding the bus, Dorothy gave her jacket to Ashley, telling him she wouldn't need it, much to the objection of the busload. We all felt she would need it, at least at John F. Kennedy International Airport. But she was adamant, and he relented. Elaine said, "You sure you want to do this?"

I continued to feel and be a part of every place I've visited. That's why having the newspapers and CNN are a must for me.

I was home for seven days before I headed off to Barbados.

I was met at the airport as usual and began to thaw out and relax by the time we reached Bernita Apartments. I picked up a few breakfast groceries, settled into my apartment, and then began to soul-search (or should I say meditate?). I refused a dinner invitation to purposely take the time plus the next day to review last year's life changes and looked forward to Lovett, Mary, Dorothy, and whomever else might come on down.

I thought about Bill's phone calls over the months since Elaine, Onaje, and I drove to Syracuse in '89, purposely so he could see and talk with his grandson. I should have taken a picture of those three look-alikes. His last call was to inform me of his diabetes. This was no surprise. I had warned him of his family heritage and his total disregard of his diet. He left his family in Syracuse and lived alone in the best single housing he could afford as a veteran and that Elaine, with her political connections, would allow. He continued to describe me as "his best friend."

Back to the snow and cold—home sweet home with family and friends. I continued my twice-a-week swim at the YMCA with Dorothy, picked up work from the State Social Work Board, and accepted membership on the board for a four-year term. I met with Evelyn Williams at Whitney Young to discuss a constitution and supervision contract to plan for social work in-house and outreach within each department. One of our potential interns at Carver would be attending Syracuse University for her graduate degree, having permission from her school, but needed a licensed supervisor at her placement. If I accepted her, this called for meeting her faculty advisor for lunch. She had been an exceptional undergrad while working at Carver Day Care, so I had no question about her capabilities as a graduate student.

As summer brought Onaje home, August seemed to be the time for the party to celebrate Elaine's appointment as assistant deputy commissioner in the retirement department, her birthday and mine, plus summer.

We traveled to Syracuse and met with Bill's other family at the hospital where he was in the first stage of rehab following foot surgery. His plan was to go to a VA hospital. I know he could feel Elaine's frustration, which was all the more reason to enjoy relatives, friends, food, fun, and open doors.

August 31 brought a phone call to supervise two MSWs at the Life Start Program in Schenectady. Each received an hour at this alcohol/drug program that had been developed by a lawyer who seemed to have a good handle on what outreach rehabilitation should entail. More than ever, my practice was taking me away from my own office and away from Albany. The Schenectady Christ Church Day Care had a social worker who needed supervision. Would I consider this for next year? Sure. Why not?

A visit from Birdie before he left for England was a good excuse for another party. He could tell everyone all about Benita Apartments, and friends and family could see the person who would have liked me to marry him and live in Barbados. With Dorothy and Ashley, he felt quite at home, since they were both West Indian. He shopped at Sears for garden tools, had them shipped, and was on his way. He would see me in Barbados. My apartment would be as usual, and neighbors the same.

As I closed down that year, I felt I had to respond to a legislator's notice of public hearings relative to strengthening and preserving families. After citing the lack of positive communication between provider and consumer and lack of basic education and respect, an attitude both carry, he then said, "It is what it is. Train and build together. More money is not the answer." I felt gratified by the response from Senator Hoyt and left for Barbados on a high.

My first action upon returning home was to call Mary Savage to offer my condolences and perhaps get some information about John's illness. The exchange was short. "He spoke of you often and thought so much of you." She promised to send a copy of the ceremony, wished me well, and hung up. Needless to say, I never received the program. We had been discussing and trying to accept each other's goals since my retirement. As John received a transfer from Westchester to the Comstock facility, he rented a house in Glens Falls, joined a church in Saratoga, and received permission to establish an NAACP chapter in Saratoga and one at the prison. When asked, I participated in the workshops and received letters of thanks from the phase-out reentry group. Eventually John accepted my decision not to marry and move permanently to Glens Falls and would call me to have coffee breaks with him as he drove down to Westchester—back to his family I never knew.

I saw how bad the winter had been and continued to be as water damaged two upstairs rooms, destroyed my "Manhattan Skyline" twenty-five-hundred-piece framed puzzle. Ice and snow clogged the gutters. This was the final door to another adventure. I started having "porch sales," put the house on the market, and, with Elaine, planned my scaled-down future living. Elaine spent several years as a rental agent while juggling her professional career, sandwiched between son and mother, She chose and continued her work back home in Albany, structuring the campaign and working with the Albany County DA. She sold her Bronx condo. Together we looked at various two-family houses, but I was finished with remodeling, decorating, and so forth. I wanted apartment living and, having explored available new facilities. I got back to my original choice. I moved into a two-bedroom, two-bath apartment with a balcony in Colonie.

My private practice consisted of 80 percent consultation, supervision, and program development in Schenectady and with Whitney Young in Albany. Individual and family cases came from the County DSS.

Our August picnic parties seemed to be someone being replaced each year by a member of the Barbados group, especially Eleanor Nottingham. Although she lived in Connecticut, we met in Barbados. We were both from Long Island and we shared a family doctor, Doctor Granger, but most importantly, we shared a love for the sea. Looking over the albums, I saw that most of us were in swim-suits at one time or another, but El and I were the only swimmers and slot players.

In addition to yearly summer gatherings, I began to have Bajan visitors. One couple from our Partners of the Americas group was impressed by the sights, but particularly by the nature of our diverse relationships and living arrangements. Roslyn Jordan, a social worker who was now in law school, came to discuss a domestic-violence project she wanted to implement after she graduated.

The project that I designed, structured, and set in motion was bringing a young theatrical group to meet other "Partners" members: Professor Mars Hill, writer and producer of numerous plays; the director and members of Capital Rep; members of the Links; and a tour of the city. Partners brought an adult choir to Albany for a concert when the Albany-Barbados affiliates first started so that it would seem that the mission was being accomplished.

I walked from Grand Central to Park Avenue, feeling complete, happy, and energized to attend our semiannual New York State Social Work board meeting in the city. The many family and friend celebrations, whether weddings, births, funerals, graduations, anniversaries, plus my work and organization involvement, each and all made up my persona.

As I remembered my very early childhood and teen years, I felt joy and completeness. I accepted this abundant life. I continued to meet new people, places, and opportunities with open, faithful arms, which seemed to attract and set off a challenge to male friends. As Booker and I went to several concerts, holiday celebrations, and attended a church where he sang, I refused to give up my work or club work to become his helpmate as he said Christ ordered. I thought, here we go again. Christ didn't ask this of women. No, in fact he accepted Mary Magdalene as another disciple to spread his teachings. Even taking Booker to Carver's Christmas party to meet the people and learn what the programs were all about made no difference to him. "Anybody can do that work," he said.

It was good to hear from Barbara's friends as I took a Pavarotti tape for Helen and me to listen to at Albany County Nursing Home. Then I enjoyed my movies with Onaje and visits with Ella before taking my yearly leave from my consulting agencies and heading to the big island again. However, the ongoing loss of friends and the crippling illnesses that brought about changes in our activities brought about the realization that I must boost my interaction with them as well as with new people—Izetta, Helen, Gladys, Lester, Ralph, Martha, and Parker, my long-time and recent friends and family members. All seemed to leave before I had a chance to receive them and laugh at old times together.

Gladys made a trip to Barbados one year, and we shared memories back to the forties, when we worked in the Tax Department. Our other pinochle partners had since died. Both Links and M. C. Lawton's had lost members, necessitating stronger recruitment efforts to fulfill their service missions. At Carver, Michael Henderson was appointed temporary director while the board members acted as if this was "access time."

Onaje transferred from Buffalo State to Xavier in New Orleans—keeping physics, calculus, and engineering uppermost in his future. This transfer of schools afforded my girlfriend Isabel and me the added venture to New Orleans. We attended the Black Child Development Conference; toured the campus and riverfront; and took a gambling cruise to Mobile, Alabama. Back home, as Links, we discussed extending her successful annual "Honoring the Black Family" program by soliciting names of people from the community. We videotaped our interviews and presented these oral histories to school libraries, and so forth. What a major successful project for bringing together community, school, and national organization of Links.

The success of this project was the effort of Isabel and Link president, Nanette Ashe, who set up the priority for the organization. My contact with the School of Social Welfare brought further support and exposure. Elaine gave voice as the program announcer and provided another linkage level.

As this three-year project got underway, and Schenectady work picked up, a new Family Preservation Program director asked for more hours of supervision for the entire program staff. Whitney Young asked for supervision for an outreach person from the multiaddiction service. As I listened to the directors of both Schenectady and Albany programs, I surmised that the board of directors didn't seem to be functioning well. One board had no committees; the director was in charge and "reported program business to the board." Another had an overzealous membership that interfered with the daily decision-making of various programs. Neither seemed to accept the annual workshops sponsored by the United Way or Council of Community Services. My discussion with the directors ended with thanks and a request for time on the boards. My response was, "I'd be glad to serve on your program committee when I retire."

It was summertime, and we were on the road to Islesford, Maine, to visit Dartmouth Professor Ashley at the lobster festival. We drove the Delaware Bridge Tunnel, in spite of being exhausted and being asked by the passengers that we take the highway home. We were on the road to explore the Underground Railroad route, the last stop for the escaped slaves before they sailed home to

Africa. LaVerne, Eleanor, Dorothy, and I drove to Halifax, Nova Scotia, to discover the last settlement of free or escaped slaves. The current population was so welcoming; they have a tourism business. I asked the directors to present their history at our annual Underground Railroad conference—the names of the early settlers, the first AME Church and members, and, most importantly, why some chose to stay while others went back home. What an education.

I thought of the Native American, who had nowhere to go. The black Indian had choices. I remember the picture of the Indian with his canoe having come overland from Connecticut or Massachusetts to Mastic Beach on the southern shore of Long Island and seeing only the great Atlantic ahead of him.

Another trip to New Orleans offered the opportunity to celebrate a family get-together as Onaje graduated from Xavier and a visit to Storyville for dinner and jazz. Neither Howard nor I could believe the food, two rooms of jazz, and lunch after graduation at the "House of Blues," the museum featuring "The Thinker." What a venture! We also met the Alpha brothers and the future Mrs. Harper, all of whom would have been lost to me if I had not taken pictures.

As I was "all clear" following gallbladder surgery, I accompanied Ella to her many doctor appointments until she was told, "We can't do anymore for you. Melanoma has no cure." We got a second opinion with the same results, so Ella decided to live her life as she chose, with company and beer. Her only regret was that she turned in her driver's license.

At the same time, niece Loris had been ordered to get a series of tests relative to ongoing walking and back problems. She called or visited periodically, feeling good about her love life, but was stubborn about not discussing the relationship with her daughters. This was so hurtful for me. I even suggested to her father, whom she loved dearly, that perhaps he might help her to understand that she needed to demand more from the girls. She wouldn't accept a referral for family counseling. In the meantime, she suffered physically.

Loris visits Helen at home, Jay Street

As another late August arrived, Elaine, Onaje, and I, celebrated by seeing *Ragtime* on Broadway, and then went on to Huntington to have birthday dinner with Elsie and Marge while Elaine was serenaded by a mariachi band in the Mexican restaurant. It seemed that my quiet meditation prayer time was dwindling as the adventure in living, interacting with people, and seeing new places was pushing the twenty-four hours. Still, having been cleared by the cardiologist and primary doctors, I rescheduled my volunteer hours to accept two one-year projects with the understanding that I'd be away during January and February.

The Covent Charter School, developed by the Urban League, was a board I chose to be on so I could negotiate space at the city-owned Arbor Hill Community Center. Who would build and operate the pool? The nominations committee revealed how many board members lacked my knowledge of board structure, time rotations, and how members were solicited. I then understood why Aaron accepted my conditions. "If my name will be of help on the application, then I will do it for one year only."

My other adventure was to accept the weekly meeting with the students in the Liberty Partnership "Millennium Elders Project." These great high scholars were challenged to interview family elders about their experience growing up. Senior students hesitated to approach "older folks," their excuse being, "They're not like us, and they don't like us." After several sessions with them on approaching their elders, no matter where or how, by phone or in church, I found several who were visibly distressed about the project. All had to be convinced that a known friend or church elder would satisfy the requirement. Another had a grandparent of another ethnicity and, added to that "problem," the student felt distant from classmates since, "I play the violin, and that's not cool." I immediately felt his need for assurance, counseling, guidance, and self-esteem building.

Once the students identified their elder to interview and write about, the director gave the guidelines, time constraints, and the project closing as school closed with a banquet and show.

The director was pleased that my condition for being an interviewed elder helped her student. He was now more a part of the group and seemed to enjoy being with other students, teachers, and faculty. For me, having to focus on my school days and my feelings about the experiences was extraordinary—only surpassed by meeting other elders from the Arbor Hill area at the program closing, including grandparents and church folks I hadn't seen in over thirty years. We ate dinner and enjoyed the students' performances, directed by Mark Bob Semple.

These feel good times balanced the reality of family members' illnesses and deaths. I relived those depressive days: feeding Evelyn by spoon, and coaxing Loris to sign her state insurance papers. While I was encouraged by George and Howard's physical stabilization at this time and that each of us had a child keeping tabs on our needs, supporting us as they "sandwiched" their lives. As I rejoiced with Elaine on her Revson Fellowship award from Columbia, I challenged the faculty at Smith College in support of Janice's charge of their overlook and dismissal of racism actions by a student. Correspondence and meetings with the dean brought about several major changes.

Eleanora suggested that this summer's Barbados gang attend the annual Penn Center Heritage Day celebration at Saint Helena Island, South Carolina. This called for some real organizing. She was willing to host at her home. LaVerne arrived from Greensboro, North Carolina, and Dorothy and I drove from Albany to her home in Wilmington, North Carolina. My rented car gave me problems for the last few miles, so Eleanora got us to her garage, and she drove the rest of the trip, except over the bridge to South Carolina. I couldn't understand this phobia. Neither Eleanora nor Dorothy nor LaVerne would tackle it. For me, just being able to get to the islands was enough incentive to overcome any challenges it brought. The bridge's height and the sea beneath it were beautiful. What an educational and fun day. Penn Center was the education center for emancipated slaves.

I had heard of the Geechies, African descendants of Sierra Leone, Liberia, Gambia, and Senegal who reside on coastal South Carolina and Georgia. This was their home, language, culture and world. Storytellers, artists, musicians, and culinary arts (my first taste of fried turkey). However, I was back home as a child with the oysters and fish plates. As if I hadn't experienced enough, Isabel and I, representing our Link chapter to continue our national focus on the aging, went to the United Nations session "Toward a Society for All Ages." It was overwhelming to be seated in that huge assembly room, close to the guest speakers' podium. Family and friends must have grown tired of my story of the UN, Eleanor Roosevelt, my trip, and my hopes of returning to that powerful, historic world site.

I celebrated another gratifying Thanksgiving with Elaine. This year was shared with Agnes and her daughter, Janet. I recalled the previous year at Old Westbury as Elaine gave us the grand tour of the campus, her cottage, friends, and sharing over dinner. Oh, how I needed the glow of this parting year, as 2011 started with Loris "having a bone problem and scheduled for a biopsy. Of course I went to Barbados from January 9 to March 6.

The American Airlines strike forced my extra time away. My frustration led me to start writing short memoirs until I finally got home to work full-speed ahead on the Links' Legacy Project and State Board meeting and Office of Professional Discipline cases. The Family Preservation Program's director at Carver became seriously ill. I was asked to extend my days. How could I refuse? So, instead of one day, it became three days. I was quite aware that, at the time, the Carver director was looking to consolidate the alcoholism program with family preservation and move the program to State Street. It took all of my evening meditation to focus on "Let it go. Retirement is for letting go. You've done your job."

I took Loris to Albany Medical Center for her chemotherapy treatments, and then admittance. I felt totally helpless; with all my professional and relationship skills, family love, and togetherness, I was unable to stop her daughters from arguing. They couldn't be in the same room with her together. We celebrated Loris's life and passing on September 10. As I lay in bed watching the *Today Show*, I was struck with horror and disbelief, as I watched the attack on the Twin Towers. It was all I could do to get out of bed to call Elaine, who would hopefully not be near downtown Manhattan.

She reached me later and described the horror as she drove over the Brooklyn Bridge into downtown Manhattan. Like the rest of America, I was glued to the TV whenever possible for the next thirty days. To me, it was the most extreme demonstration of anger. "We will make you acknowledge us." Those young hijackers, to me, were operating with the same "love and loyalty" to their countries as our Volunteer National Guard.

A lovely Saratoga wedding and my weekly singing group helped to make real the goodness of my life. The lingering odor from the horror met us as we emerged from Grand Central Station to walk over toward Park Avenue where the State Social Work board meeting was held. By this time, as the Carver, Whitney Young, Link Legacy interviewing and church duties continued, my mind, as usual, was on Barbados. One morning, I found myself at Troy Family Court responding to a call from Loris's daughter that her seven-year old had torn up her classroom, throwing books, papers, and anything she got her hands on. The school called her mother and Social Services. As I listened to the counselor discuss prior and future support for mother and daughter, it brought to mind the years of generational disconnect between George's family members and, most of all, the issue of accepting and understanding professional counseling. I shared that with them, got Daj to say how she missed her grandmother, and explained that there were other family members who cared for her as well. I think that in her effort to demonstrate "this is my life," her mother found herself and family needing and provided for those needs. Total retirement—oh, yes.

I shuffled off to Barbados for just a few weeks as the Link Legacy Project was presented at the State Museum. Meetings and dates were set for other showings. These were such busy, positive times with members and community. I committed to edit the Legacy Videos in preparation for publishing them with the help of SUNY School of Social Welfare.

Eleanora and friends who were spending a jazz weekend at Friar Tuck in the Catskills rescued me. I was grateful for the support and joy in my life, as another family member passed, and a close, lately developed friend, Marie Bennekin, died.

I, along with Betty and the newly incorporated board of Arbor Hill Community Center were committed to making a success of the new programs. Although we disagreed on the approach to some issues, we moved it along. As she had organized the Democratic club in Arbor Hill, she was a powerful influence on many issues. When I left the board, we remained friends. We drove to Martha's Vineyard to visit my childhood friend Vera and spent a week in Barbados, which revealed to me just how much in control and powerful she felt when she clashed with Mary and Dorothy. Earlier in the day, I told her to stop calling me "Ma."

How joyful the year, despite other losses—cousin Grace at 101 years old and Annabel Puels. Elaine took a vacation to Brazil, and, in December, the pending union of Onaje and Katrina was celebrated in the city at BB King's House of Blues and Brunch. No one but Elaine and I danced to "Celebration." As I took the train back to Albany, I thought of what the future year would be with my vacation, the wedding, and whether or not I should or would return from Barbados to accept the Martin Luther King Humanitarian Award.

During the icy snowy days that began '03, I looked forward to sun, sand, and sea. I knew I must return to honor the Links, and particularly Isabel, who did the work of researching and writing a biographical sketch that resulted in my being the New York State awarder in this category.

The support I received in making this decision from the Links, to Elaine driving to the city for pick up and return, to understanding my inability to "walk the beloved community wreath laying ceremony," to Linda hosting the luncheon reception. What a great day. Family, Links, Lawtons, and friends. But it was so cold. I returned to Barbados where the Almond Tree gang had a huge bouquet and congratulations for me.

Eleanora and I planned our wardrobe possibilities for the wedding before she returned to the United States. Upon my return, it seemed as though Schenectady's court system, social services, and Ellis Hospital Emergency were in conflict with their own purposes. I spent longer than usual—extra days getting specific case problems—targeting possible solutions and who should be involved. The United Way, via the New Carver director, notified the program director of several dates that one of their staff would be at the facility to check the records. I had to remind all involved of confidentiality. The families distrusted the system—they wanted to know if they were going to become a part of this historical pattern when, in fact, all that was needed was a statistical analysis of their cases. That should satisfy the funding sources without divulging personal information. I had to keep my cool as I attributed this and other problems to a "rubber-stamp board" whose director "didn't need committees." He would let the board know how the programs were functioning. No finances, program, building and grounds, or publicity.

In mulling this over I concluded that my job from now on would be to support, strengthen, and train the program director toward using statistical reports, sent monthly to board meetings with enough copies for all, as well as to the United Way. I informed her that I would probably retire in 2005 from all work. However, I could consider being on the board or doing board work.

Mulling over this final decision helped me to decide how much involvement I wanted that called for teaching, supervision, and reports. I had professional-discipline meetings and phone conferences periodically; one fall evening SUNY community organization class as substitute instructor; and any call from Whitney Young, for whatever emergency. I could sleep, write, visit, walk the malls, swim, and be with family and friends.

Onaje and Katrina's wedding in the garden in New Orleans was storybook. I was unable to attend Howard and Mary's wedding in Maryland, but I celebrated as if I were there.

I sat in the sun with Ella that summer and early fall, exchanging the latest news of home, gossip, and hearsay and commenting about our large family roots that was now populating Albany as well, both in the south end and on the Hill. Did I deserve so much? I sat in the Texas sun with Onaje and Katrina and with Velma in the Florida sun for two weeks before visiting LaVerne in North Carolina.

Then I got the news of another family member's passing. Ella was now under hospice care, and George was hospitalized. He came home to pass in mid-June. It was difficult holding his hand, watching him struggle between acknowledging the requests of his children. "Coffee, Dad? What TV show do you want to watch? You want lunch?" And then, he just drifted off to meet Evelyn. As the hospice doctor explained George's state to his children. I became "Aunt Cissie, what shall we do?"

I was happy for him but concerned about Howard. What would the introvert do without his other half? He had been to see George but left before I got there. We needed each other now as we made arrangements for his passing and the what, where, and when were the problems. Then who rode with whom in the procession became a major issue for family.

I became interested in the county DA campaign, as a challenger was black, and Elaine had been approached to train the volunteers. I made phone calls and was most overjoyed at his installation ceremony. The next day, I was on my way to Wilmington, North Carolina, to spend a week with Eleanora, who had suffered from a stroke. We, along with her daughter, enjoyed the warm fall days riding along the shore.

I had been back in Albany for three days when I got the call from El in the hospital. We sang her favorite Rod Stewart song. She passed that night. It had been an eight-year developing friendship.

I felt strengthened by Elaine's being in Albany and asked her to enrich the community organization class I had committed to. What an uplift both the students and I got from her sharing and adding to their knowledge of how local program needs relate and are processed through city, county, state and federal funding sources.

We planned for the Thanksgiving and Christmas with Howard, Agnes, Janet, Linda, and Bill. No Barbados. I couldn't think of being at the apartment, knowing that Eleanora, Mary, Dorothy, and Margaret would not be part of the season's experience.

Dorothy was hospitalized for knee replacement. As the year progressed, I wondered how I would have felt coming home to hear that Emily Grissom, Marion Hughes, and Joyce Drysdale had passed. Dot returned to the hospital for readjustment of the knee replacement.

How strange to be home in the snow and cold, attending a Martin Luther King program at the Convention Center, visiting and cooking for Ella, and attending the "going home" ceremonies.

Spring was late, but welcomed, as Judy and I met to plan and draft our booklet *Counting the Cost of Caring*. Over the years, she had continued to bring me up to date on her life. I praised her for including the care of parents with Alzheimer's along with her own husband and four children. We agreed that caretakers pay physical and psychological costs when their natures are caring. After suffering from panic attacks and several hospitalizations, perhaps writing would add to her return to health, along with her faith and church work.

My weekly sessions at Carver became lengthier, as if these last months could provide the knowledge for all subsequent cases. As the summer ended with Elaine's birthday party at the Japanese restaurant, I went on a trip to Dallas that took me back to my teen jazz years by being with Onaje and Katrina in the Brooklyn Jazz Club. Walking the huge outdoor mall was joyous. I needed those great summer feelings as the family gathered for Ella's funeral and memorial. Her grandchildren were so lost and at odds with each other as we older family members did our best to support them individually. The Long Island members stressed the need for them to know where their original home was and to consider a change.

How blessed I was to say to my Carver group, "I've enjoyed every day with you—my phone and home are open to you." We had a wonderful lunch and I received gifts galore. As I drove home, I thanked God to have seen this day—total retirement from work. I was eighty-two years old.

I read, slept, and socialized while performing organization and committee work. I went to Saratoga, Yonkers, Belmont, and Foxwood with Isabel; Long

Island with Elsie, Marge, Mary, Richie, and whoever were still there—had lunch and made trips to Walmart with Dot and her live-in-helper or daughter. What a great scheduling time. I was cognizant of new commitments, such as responding to and arranging for the Links Legacy members to make guest appearances throughout the community.

Having seen their video, the director of Whitney Young Health Center wanted a similar video of as many of their founders as possible to be part of a dinner celebration, and we had weekly exchange visits. Howard and I, remembering our journeys, and those along the way. We exchanged favorite mystery books for my baked marble cake.

Instead of Barbados, I visited Onaje and Katrina in Dallas, enjoyed the Bajans who visited Partners members during the summer, which was much cooler here than at home. But, I was determined to go to Barbados next year. How overjoyed I was when Elaine agreed to accompany me to see the Barbados that I enjoyed. So off we went, staying at Miami Beach apartments—home. Everyone was glad to see her. We went to Findlay's concert. We met, dined, and were driven home by a resident Caucasian couple living down the highway from where we resided.

We were at the beach by day and the variety of restaurants by night. Gloria, Deb, Elaine, and I lingered over dinner and music at one of the newer eateries, overlooking the sea. I reluctantly returned home in March. Elaine spent ten days. Gloria and Deb's timeshare was for three weeks, so we met several times before I was alone with my Barbados family. I thought about the twenty-four-year experience and realized that more than a vacation, this experience each year not only allowed me to be me, twenty-four hours a day, seven days a week, it supported and intensified my work with organizations as well as in professional consultations.

I attended a special Albany meeting of the State Social Work Board to discuss certification exams, which the director of the national boards and the deans of colleges conferring master's degrees also attended. This was heavy. I couldn't pass up the opportunity, since so many of the black social-work graduates didn't pass or refused to try the exams. While I was there, The dean invited me to the first Diversity Conference ever held by SUNY with deans and faculty from all over the country on May 7. She had been instrumental in setting it up. I accepted and looked forward to being stimulated by new outside thinkers.

I drove to the new science building, parked, and made my way into the building via newly constructed, but incomplete, sidewalks. I stumbled and went down. With help, I brushed myself off and joined the group. I entered, registered, and accepted coffee from staff who had witnessed the accident. I was seated in the front row, ready to hear the keynote speaker, followed by workshops. At the lunch break, I tried to stand, but such pain, as I'd never felt before, put me back on the chair, crying out. I got the diagnosis—a fractured pelvis bone.

A had to adapt to a new lifestyle, supported and encouraged by family and friends. The recuperation, both physical and mental, was constantly fed by faith and prayer.

Yes, a new life and recognition of age in terms of physical wear and tear over my eighty-four years. And although I would have liked to accompany our Link Believers and achievers on the trip to the United Nations and walk the mall at Afro American Family Day, I had to be grateful for a wealth of support as I confronted these limitations and having Howard along the way. I've come to accept the last chapter of immediate family life, following the loss of Howard in the spring of '09. I felt alone, but not lonely. Then I was blessed with a great-granddaughter to remind me that the beat goes on—Elaine, Onaje, and Kiera.

*You never really leave
a place you love. Part of it
you take with you, leaving
a part of yourself behind.*
—Anonymous

BARBADOS:
THE DOVER BEACH YEARS

From the time we touched down in Barbados on January 15, 1983, to this day, Mary and I confirm it as our natural habitat. It became my second freedom. We spent ten to fourteen days at the Gap in Bresmay, Time Out, and Carib Blue, all of which are on Dover Beach along with a variety of restaurants, grocery stores, slot-machine rooms, and taxi stands. One block up from the Carib Blue was the main highway. Buses ran regularly and, later, privately owned, licensed vehicles that accommodated up to six people serviced the latecomers. The eastern end of the Gap led us past an exclusive, gated resort, which provided private taxi service for its guests, and then onto a great Italian restaurant on the main road.

The western end of the Gap led past the Dive, the Silver Fox massage parlor, and the Marlin Coffee and Cream art gallery and jewelry store. And at the top of the hill, was her husband, David's, restaurant. At this end of the Gap, the main road led to the Town of Saint Michael. We took every island tour and accepted the cordial invitations from residents, both native and dual residents. Each year, a previous travel friend accompany us. These short yearly visits were not enough for me. Subsequently an open door! An introduction to the tourism associations and the U.S. programs Partners of the Americas held at the Turf Inn featuring buffet and resort and housing owners distributing brochures. The Bernita Apartments suited my budget, and situated a block from the bus stop. It was three miles away from the Gap and Dover Beach. It had amenities such as, airport pickup, weekly grocery trips and apartment maintenance. What more could I ask for?

From '85-'95 Apartment 1 was mine. I was retired. No need to limit vacation time. I eventually extended my freedom, encouraging other friends and family to visit. I learned so much from this branch of my journey. For instance, when my friend Gladys and I were checking in at the airport, she was turned away due to lack of birth certificate or passport. She called me that night and informed me that her sister had the family Bible in which all births were recorded in North Carolina. So she would be joining me within the next two days. Bertie Chase, who managed the facility would not only meet all the new visitors, but also drop by to talk periodically and make introductions with others in the 11-apartment complex. The other apartment was called "the cave." It was carved and finished into a huge living area complete with kitchen, bedroom, shower, and entertaining area. No windows were necessary as the opaque ceiling provided light and shelter from the torrential rain. Mr. Chase ("Call me Bertie") began to visit the apartments daily and spent more time in my apartment. I worked my two-thousand-piece jigsaw puzzle, and he gave me pieces of his life. He had been married twice. His first wife, a nurse, drowned. He had a daughter he was very close to, who lived in St. John parish. His second wife lived in the United States with their two sons. Their divorce was pending.

Each year, as we were driven from the airport, Mary asked, "How have you been? How's your love life?" To which Bertie related his latest trials and dating issues. He was always on the verge of remarriage. Our friendships grew as sisters. Link invited Mary and me to have lunch with her bridge-club friends. Although we didn't play bridge, we enjoyed meeting those who had either married Bajan men and moved to the island or were retired US workers returned to their homeland.

Thelma introduced me to the International Women's Club, which held monthly meetings at the Hilton Hotel, located near Bridgetown, the capital. The group held an annual international fair that Mary and I attended one year. What an education to meet people from other nations, especially Cubans, and taste such a variety of food. Each year I, along with Dorothy or Ellen, visited Thelma, who was in her nineties. Her younger relatives insisted that she either move back to the United States with them or into a nursing home—senior housing on the island. I connected with her at a line assembly in 2006. She was wheelchair-bound and cared for by her niece. The next year, I visited with her in a Barbados nursing home. Following my physical handicap, I only learned of Thelma's demise by way of Lovette—another prior Westchester County Link.

After seeing Mary off at the airport, I took the bus back to Bernita Apartments. While waiting at the bus stop, a pleasant young woman approached, asking if I was a visitor. We struck up an immediate friendship as she offered to meet the next day and give me a tour of Bridgetown—library, stores, slots, and eateries. Beverly was like my Elaine—another daughter. She worked at the duty-free shop at the airport from eight to four; lived with Mike; and loved music, books, and slot machines. As I shared my travel experiences with her, she educated me about her island and its people.

After visiting my apartment, we walked to the beach. She said, "The road we are walking on was off-limits to us until recently. Most of these homeowners are dual-citizen folks and returning nationals. We're considered British subjects." I reaffirmed this as a tour director later directed our attention to a beautiful home being built by Tony Blair for his retirement. I had dinner with Beverly and Mike, and we took trips into northern areas of previous plantations—now used for tobacco, corn, and other marketable vegetables and fruit. I made sure that all of my visitors had a chance to meet Beverly and Mike and, eventually, little Bryan.

My relationship with Joanne continued to feel like sisterhood.

Onaje, at sixteen, was having a first taste of being overwhelmed by girls. We had dinner at Boomers in the Gap, where teenage waitresses teased him and competed with each other for his attention. The university campus president and faculty gave him a warm welcome as well as Dorothy and me as members of Partners of the Americas. Tony and Madelyn, in apartment four, encouraged him to walk the beach with them.

I inadvertently dropped our passports, cash, plane tickets, and keys on a bench near the shore a mile back. Our bus driver understood my panic and the emergency. He let us off the bus and awaited our return.

Prior to boarding that tour bus in Bridgetown, I made a purchase and had two bags on my arm. As the tour bus approached the water side of the island, we made a stop. Onaje and I walked the beach, snapped pictures of the three sisters (huge rocks along the shore), and I rested at a picnic table. For some reason, I removed my bag and placed it on the table. The Albany High track-team leader waved the bag as he started back up the hill to where I had made it on the road between the banana trees. The bus crowd smiled and clapped while I thanked the driver and commented, "This wouldn't happen in New York."

Each year brought a new adventure. I became acquainted with brother George's brother-in-law, Jeremiah Parsons, who was walking with USAID stationed in Barbados. He came by while Marie Benson was visiting and took us to the pottery barn. His workstation while he was home was Chalky Mount. Each time we went out, Marie said, "I'm sitting in front."

Then, while coming from the grocery in Holetown, Dorothy, Mary, Marlin, and I overloaded the taxi with bundles of food. She called to me and I replied, "Please don't call me Mom. I'm not your mother." We all laughed and got our taxi home, where each volunteered to be responsible for some part of dinner since we were eating in at my apartment. Mary volunteered to cook the chicken, Marie to make dessert, Dorothy a big salad, and I provided drinks and set up.

Mary rushed upstairs. "She's taking the skin off the chicken, Frazier. Who ever heard of chicken without skin?" Mary responded just as hastily, "You want skin, I'll give you skin. Here! Cook it." Mary wouldn't eat with us that night, but the broiled chicken, rice, salad, and cake she made were delicious. Mary joined us for poker and talk.

I was free once more as I saw each one leave, allowing me two weeks to assess what happened. Was it a bad mix, or was it me? I had little time to delve into it, as Bertie and neighbors dropped by to keep me company. Bertie started off with, "I need to find out what my problem is with women. I've learned all I know about them from TV's *Days of Our Lives*, but it's not working. I can't get my divorce, and Barbara isn't satisfied with our arrangement, even though she gets paid the same."

He no longer considered the Bible or Christianity as his backup. I began to believe his desperation, his longing to be closer to his sons, and the need to have someone share responsibility of the property. I listened and stated my understanding about the business yet pointed out that he had made some personal choices and seemed to be waiting for some female to rescue him. He talked about his trip to England, visiting old friends and staying with Bonita and her husband. They treated him royally and agreed that Bonita would visit soon. As a former teacher, I suspected there had to be some "status" issues involved, as well as gender issues. I recalled, my mother's comments about *The Guiding Light* and *Days of Our Lives*: "These men are all alike. They think they know everything."

I was anxious to return to my schedule of Dover Beach swimming, reading, dinner, slots with Beverly, and jazz at the Time Out. However, I was not about to start working, so I got directly to the point with Bertie the next day—his knowledge and concern about age; physical health; management of the apartments; finances; and, most devastating of all, the separation from his church, the historic "Case Home." Suggesting that he take notes, I had him list positive corrective outcomes that he felt able to accomplish. Several persons before me had suggested he build a pool to accommodate nonsea swimmers, bargain with his sons—who better to manage their inheritance?—apologize to whomever necessary, and get on with taking care of his aging mind and body. And get back to his church since, according to him, he put soul, body, energy, and finances there to continue a family legacy. The elementary approach worked.

He met me as I arrived back from my daily beach excursion saying that he had spoken with his eldest son who seemed enthused about the idea. He spoke as if this would solve all his problems. He could now find out if Barbara was faring well. He let the visitor's desk at the airport know that he would return calls immediately and needed to update schedules on incoming flights. The next morning, before I could make the beach, he knocked and entered. "This time it's going to be right. I deserve it. The Lord knows that getting a housemate will answer my problems, no matter how long Barbara holds up the divorce." He pounded his fist into his hand while looking at me for approval or confirmation.

I cautioned him against hasty actions without discussion with the person involved and listening to what is being said.

Upon returning from Dover, I met my new neighbor who had to spend the first week of her vacation in an unfamiliar parish of Barbados because no one answered the airport traveler's aide call about the arrival of a guest. That evening, we got acquainted. She enlightened all of us about Rudy, her friend, who was separated from her husband, Bertie Chase. She understood why her friend took the boys to the United States while she pursued her teaching career. "The island life is tough for women—we can't challenge the men in any way."

The next day, Dot A. mentioned that we might have to look for other apartments next year. I agreed as I searched the so-called brochure—R. Chase, owner, with the embassy in her address and just a phone number for Bernita Apartment's manager.

No problem. I just had to be careful as I packed my sea fern to take home with me, after seven years in my window, holding down the fort for me.

The next several days were so perfectly relaxing. No drama, no mice, no giant grasshoppers, just the beach, slots, dinners, talk with neighbors, and finishing a puzzle.

Two weeks before leaving, I opened my balcony door, I heard, "Hello, Florence. I'm Bernita, It's my birthday, and we just got back from church. We'll see you later." Sure enough, before I left for an afternoon with Beverly and Mike, B and B came to the apartments with loud greetings. She seemed genuinely interested in our recommendations to improve the apartments, keeping in mind that having been built out from the coral, there would be "creatures" poking their heads out from time to time, as well as greenery. I left with Mike and Beverly, ready for a relaxing afternoon with this young couple. Their lower apartment and garage faced the main highway seven.

I learned that Bev had an eye for decoration as well as being an avid reader. Her library of mysteries was extensive. Mike was totally into sports via television. Both had left large families—Beverly's in the country, Mike's in Bridgetown. A blue-ribbon dinner as only the Bajans can offer necessitated our walking tour of the casinos before saying good-bye until next year.

I called Bertie to remind him of my leaving Wednesday. He replied, "I'm glad you reminded me. Please come over for a drink before you go."

Tuesday I toasted them, hoping their shared plans would work out. I was told, "Anytime you want to come down, with or without money, the place is yours."

In November 1994, I received a call at home at seven thirty in the evening from Bertie, who was in New York to have divorce papers served. I told him of Ashley's passing and gave him Dot's phone number. He said, "Bonita went back to England." I gave my condolences and wished him well with his sons. On December 20, at seven in the morning, he called with Christmas wishes and asked when I would be arriving.

That should have prepared me for the many issues and events that developed over the next two seasons. Food prices were higher, but vegetables and fruit not fresh or ripe. Yet, on a trip to Bridgetown I found the street vendors selling beautiful, fresh, ripe imports—IMF at work. The apartments had been repainted, but the phones were dead.

The new housekeeper, Leona, was very pleasant and curious about my puzzles. I told her my need to relax and put work and family issues behind. She said, "I do that in church." I agreed that your faith would carry you through.

Bertie offered to take me to his church as a special Martin Luther King service was to be presented by the US representative to Barbados. I accepted and, while in church, he remarked, "This celebration—the work he did was more for the people in the United States. We, here, passed that problem a while ago."

Oh my! Let it alone, Florence. He doesn't understand the inveracity of the Civil Rights message even as we heard the sermon delivered by the Moravian minister expounding on King's message to families and children's rights to be acknowledged by parents.

Bertie acknowledged that if I hadn't attended, he would have skipped this Sunday. However, I was glad I made it. He then said, "By the way, a Margaret called and left a message to call her at Melrose."

Mary came, as well as Dot A and Dot Bryan—who eventually stayed at Melrose Apartments near Margaret. Being able to explore the malls in Bridgetown, Hastings, Worthington, I could lead Margaret and whoever directly to their shopping satisfaction. Theater and late jazz music on the wharf for concerts at Claymore Hall satisfied our cultural thirst. Then there were churches to explore. My Methodist Episcopal, Mary's Baptist, Eleanor's and Barbara's Catholic, A thrill for me was watching the Concord fly in from England every Saturday. The huge plane carried the wealthy Europeans onto the island for business, vacation, or whatever.

Stopping at Carib Blue on my way home from the beach, I often chatted with owner Mrs. Maxwell. She and her husband were long acquaintances of

Bertie. She said, "He is really failing—he thinks he's invincible. What he needs is a woman up there, but he is so contrary that he lost the one person who kept the place going for him." I agreed, thinking of the positive years when Barbara was the caretaker.

Dot's statement about looking for alternative living arrangements seemed to be right on. I wrote postcards and finished my puzzle before Mary and the others arrive. There would be no time, what with tours, beach, shopping, dining, and visiting.

Beverly dropped by to visit and let me know of her unemployment—the airport was downsizing—so she'd be going back to school while she was job searching. Neighbors felt free to drop by and were glad to meet this young Bajan.

Several nights later, Wendy and Clarence came by, and Eleanora, a return visitor from the United States, joined our after-dinner balcony discussions. She introduced us to Hot Spot, a small body of water heated by a nearby refinery. Cascading over rocks, this natural pool for arthritic middle-agers was wonderful. As Dorothy B. prepared a good-bye dinner for Mary and Natalie, I reminded them of our two other neighbors, so six of us crowded around for dinner before leaving to attend a gospel concert.

Much to our surprise, we participated as a choir backup for a BBC tape of hymns to be broadcast in England sometime in August. What a hoot.

Another adventure took me to the St. James's church festival in Speightstown. I vowed to return on my own when I had more time. As we got little support from Bertie about the mice problem, we agreed to meet him and educate him on how he might systematically go about maintaining riddance of the mice. His response was, "Leona will be here. She needs time to know what the needs are in the apartments."

Walking and beach activities—slots and international women's activities—helped me deal with the prospect of living elsewhere in Barbados. Eleanora also loved to explore. As a result, mornings were spent alternating from beach to mall price comparison in view of later purchases, and then we had lunch with Dot and Carolyn.

Howard called for Elaine to tell me that Bill had died. I was ready to go home to Elaine, but, a series of calls from Ella, Elaine, Howard, and Janice encouraged me to stay put. Eleanora and Dorothy also helped to ground me as I worked through some residual hostility so that I could move forward. I remember feeling an everlasting sense of freedom. I could sell the house, and go wherever.

Then I went on to the sea and slots and games with Dot and Carolyn.

Another resident, a friend of Dot's, Ashford, came to apartment two, so we are full again. Bertie dropped by to ask how I was feeling, having heard my recent news. I let him know that my family and friends, even the new ones here, and especially my daughter, had worked through this with me. However, I wanted to know what happened with Bonita, how Lorna was different, and at what stage the divorce procedure was. Bertie said, "Well, Lorna is different. She is Guyanese. She works in New York at Mount Sinai Hospital and is loved by my family. Her children love me. They are fifteen, ten, eight, and seven years old. My divorce will be through this week, and within two weeks, I'll be married. All the big political Bajans are with me. Smitty will be best man. I'd like you to come up this evening—just you—to meet Lorna."

I cut him off, saying I would be with the group going to Holetown. There was no further discussion, as Wendy arrived with the barking of a dog, and Bertie rushed the balcony saying, "I can't let her see me here." More drama!

The festival was exceptionally good this year, with everything from farmers' markets to an artist sketching on-demand, food carts, music, and dancers. Calls from home, Janie, Howard, Elaine, and Isabel supported Elaine and me. What a blessing! When I was preparing to go home—sort clothes to leave, take, let go—I got a phone call from Thelma P. to give me the number of a Miami Beach Realtor.

For one thousand dollars per month, I could get a huge three-bedroom (two with twin beds and one with a double bed). My only reserve was my responsibility for two months and relying on others to come and fill in for their stays. Mrs. H. would let me know about the family schedule since it was my family vacation house. Of course, for me, Carib Blue was my alternative.

My last new acquaintance that season was an invitation from a cordial neighbor, Pat, across the road from Bernita Apartments. I had postponed with excuses several times, but I accepted this time. Who knew, I might not see her again. She had such a pleasant home. We shared backgrounds and her concerns for the many good "ladies," the housekeepers and others who were so ill-treated by Bertie. She also told me about her ongoing feud with him about the fence and trees separating their properties.

Eleanora and Wendy were called to join us as they approached the gate. We got home just before dark. After seeing Dot A. and Dorothy off, Eleanora and I took our last Dover Beach plunge. As Bertie came to get my luggage, Eleanora asked to ride along, so we both met Leona, who shared her nursing experience. Having children, she met Bertie's daughter while she was in school. Bertie said, "They call me Uncle Bertie, and I'll be there to work with them. I didn't have my own to work with."

Eleanora responded, "Just remember, they are not your children. Remember, I'd like to attend your wedding."

Lorna said, "Why, of course."

Eleanora and I discussed how and when she'd communicate with me as I said good-bye and good luck. I had a smooth trip home. Even at home, the summer of '95 was a constant interaction with Barbados. Eleanora reported on the wedding, which was unable to be performed at the "home church." I had calls and visits from the Barbados members of Partners of the Americas, and several calls from Bertie in New York. The last one to tell me that his daughter Denise would be in charge of the apartments while he was undergoing surgery in New York. He was calling Carmel also.

Upon arriving at Bernita Apartments, I knew that I wouldn't be staying. The grounds were unkempt, there was no hot water, and the birds and mice had taken over. Dorrice immediately came with a plumber, and I made reservations at Carib Blue for the month of February. Camilla was in apartment two and greeted me. I was thinking of the phone calls to make as I shared our situation with Wendy and Clarence at their visit for dinner. While on the phone on Sunday, I heard Camilla calling for help. As she came back from work, the frisky dog next door had dug under the fence to freedom and nipped Camilla on her leg. Fortunately, I found a doctor in a clinic near enough to attend to her wound.

After two weeks, Lovette and I went to Carib Blue. Mary would join me in mid-February wherever.

Eleanora called with a possible residence in the Miami Beach area. She has resided with them for several years after her retirement. Beverly and I visited the Enterprise-area home; talked with Mr. and Mrs. Pinkett, who gave us the key to a three-bedroom, two-story house three-quarters of a mile from their main beach apartment complexes. It was a great facility, but not for me as a loner with periodic visitors.

The available top-floor apartment in the building-two complex two blocks from the beach would be mine as of mid-February. It was one block from the highway in a neighborhood of single-story homes that were owned by locals and international returners. Within two blocks were a bank, Laundromat, hairdresser, and grocery store offering homegrown fruit, vegetables, and chickens.

After hearing my decision, Eleanora said that she would plan to be there next year. Beverly, Mike, Dorothy, Lovette, Margaret, and whoever discussed the pros and cons of Beverly's choices for self-employment. The luncheon with Thelma was quite an adventure, since she and Lovette had been Link sisters in the Westchester, New York, chapter. As Camilla left for the airport, I left for the Carib Blue. Although we exchanged phone calls and seasonal greeting cards, we never met again.

Dorrice informed me of Bertie's surgery and recuperation in New York, and I remarked, "You did a wonderful thing for your father by introducing him to your nurse friend."

She came to say good-bye and undertook my need to find other accommodations, hosting various others from home. Members of the Barbados Partners convened meetings at various locations. I attended to get a better sense of their expectations while Dorothy felt that she had done enough by sending a set of encyclopedias to an elementary school.

A picnic meeting at North Point, one on a farm with a plantation and another at the university, defined the serious needs that should be addressed by the organizations.

Moving to Miami Beach apartments was a surprisingly pleasant experience, especially having access to a library, post office, and a fast-food vendor. One block further along was the Oistins community, The major fishing port where people viewed the boats come in; unload at the markets; watch the cleaning and dressing of the fish; and order whatever, in any amount. On Friday nights, this area became the dining center for visitors throughout the island with picnic tables and music. People met others from around the world.

Mr. and Mrs. Pinkett were as helpful as Bev, Mike, Wendy, and Clarence in providing information about the Enterprise section of the southeast coast, where several hotels hosted paragliders and surfers.

Before leaving that year, I left a deposit at a first-floor apartment at Miami Beach Enterprise.

THE MIAMI BEACH YEARS

For the next ten years, I became a part of the island from North Point, Sam Lord's Castle, St. Johns, Enterprise, Oistins, Dover Beach, and the Gap, Accra to Holetown to Speightstown.

I remember taking two buses to a jazz concert that was being held in a northern, unexplored parish. There was no seating limit or food limit, just music and an overwhelming crowd. Jazz in Barbados! In the early eighties, Mary and I attended midnight jazz on the wharf, where I first heard Rudolph wailing on the tenor sax. He was later discovered by Roberta Flack, and then became a part of her world tour.

The midnight jazz traveled up to the lighthouse to after-hours on the Gap and formal affairs at Garfield Center where, to my surprise, I needed a formal gown in order to attend.

Thanks to Beverly, there was no way we would miss Luther Van Dross. She provided the gown, and I the tickets.

This was the year that Elaine and I agreed we needed to erase January and February, as I told her of Mr. Pinkett's demise. Thelma Austin fell and broke her arm and shoulder while attending the famous Sunday buffet at the Maxwell's Atlantis Hotel on the east coast. Elaine told me of Helen Strout's passing and funeral and Isabel's aneurism. She was now at home, being cared for by Anona and Link sisters.

I must have mourned during the night, as I awakened with tears. I haven't cried since being at the gravesite during Mom's funeral. I realized how dear these friends were to me.

My schedule was breakfast, read and meditated, and then walked to the beach (Dover). The next year, following Bryan's birth, as a group, we encouraged Beverly to become the chair and lounger renter at Miami Beach. Mike was enthusiastic about the plan and provided a schedule. He dropped off Bryan at day care and picked up the family at the beach when he completed work. It was a real success.

The jazz festival at Farley Hill, Garfield Center brought Earth, Wind, and Fire; George Benson; Grover Washington; and Santana. I couldn't miss January in Barbados. Later Dot and I covered the museum and the archives, where I learned that no one named Frazier would be found here. That was French. At the museum, we saw a painting of the Poyer plantation and were served tea and cookies.

The Partners group arranged a meeting to discuss needs other than cultural. Although acknowledgment was made of the encyclopedias, the young thespians' trip to Albany for a week, and Findley's noontime concert, teaching at Colymore Hall for school children a moneymaking skill development was needed. We agreed to share this message at our next Albany meeting. A Bajan member invited Dot, Margaret, Eleanor, and me to breakfast where she revealed her proposal for training police officers and other groups about rape and domestic violence. Good luck with that in a male-dominated society.

She had been a social worker who returned to school for a law degree. This proposal was her project. Good luck.

Gloria, Janet, and Deb from Albany also vacationed at the time-share that Mary and I bought into. I was beginning to feel more and more at home. At the same time, Mike's father and uncle came to the beach to invite me to dinner in Bridgetown. It was another adventure—my first visit to the city. It was a two-family apartment community where the grown children lived upstairs while the parents and elders had the first floor.

I received a surprise call from Bertie, who wanted to talk. Since I didn't go to the beach on Sundays (we tourists allowed the residents to enjoy the beach), I invited him and Lorna over. He came alone, saying, "I'm clear of cancer, and Lorna is a drug addict. She's still in New York." His divorce was still pending. I let him know how despicable the manipulations that they perpetuated as a couple—a false marriage in Barbados and the health and medical services in New York through her employer so she could get all the drugs she needed during his recovery. He cried while admitting the actions over the past several years, and then said that his oldest son was coming to live with him permanently. I supported this move. I had met Johnny on a visit years ago and assessed him as a responsible, caring person. Perhaps Bernita Apartments would come alive again with a young person managing.

Bev, Mike, and Bryan arrived for our dinner date, and I wished Bertie well as we proceeded up the hill to Chicken Rita's. A heavily wooded area at the end of an unpaved road was the home and restaurant. Beverly set up our picnic table while Bryan played with the other children in the house. Another car arrived bringing the nightly surfers who slept on the beaches, used the public showers, and dined nightly at Chicken Rita's.

We left at about eight o'clock as Bryan needed to get to bed. Since there were no lights in that area, we needed to get back to the main road. I was adamant about making that dinner trip on more than one occasion in subsequent years, although knowing Elaine's aversion to woodsy, outdoor dining, we didn't make the trip.

LaVerne, Gladys, and Barbara came to visit. Eleanora came as Barbara left. Caroline also came, and I received a call from Anona to meet for lunch at Brown Sugar. With my company gone, I went to Silver Sands Hotel for lunch and an afternoon of watching the windsurfers. Another lone adventure was to explore Pelican Village searching for the old artists and craftsmen I purchased from. The village was now a shopping mall for tourists seeking souvenirs.

The new home was in Speightstown, the northernmost town on the island. It was the original drop-off of slaves and was being built into a tourism highlight. At the time, it was only noise; cement dust; and narrow, crowded streets.

I wandered, finally locating the artists on the second floor of an ancient two-story building that housed a family that operating a restaurant on the first floor. However, the parks overlooking the sea compensated for the building chaos. As Maurice took Dorothy and me to his home in Oxward, he commented on the overall changes. There were fewer sugar-cane plantations and now there were vegetable farms, livestock(goats, sheep, and fowl). In his position as administration officer at the university, he had been a member of Partners, visited Albany a number of times, and now wanted us to meet his brother and family visiting from England. I was impressed by Maurice's cooking skills and superb jazz collection. What a feast. The best part of it all was being surprised by his fruitcake, which didn't look like my mother's or any of the others I had seen and didn't like. As I chose from a variety of desserts, what I thought was a slice of chocolate cake or a brownie was Maruice's "made from scratch" fruitcake. Not a trace of fruit showed, but it tasted delicious.

I needed little encouragement to extend my following year's vacation to two months. I should have anticipated a chain of life events that would necessitate keeping memories of that and other years.

From January 8 to 19, we enjoyed our reunion with our Bajan families and the beach routine from one to five, dinner wherever, slots, and then home by midnight. Eleanora maintained the apartment as I returned home on the nineteenth and stayed to the twenty-first to accept the New York State Martin Luther King Humanitarian Award.

When I returned to the apartment and saw the gorgeous bouquet from our beach group, I knew I was home. Before Eleanora left, we saw Al Jerau in concert at the gym and Santana at Farley Hill, and had celebration at Chicken Rita's. Dot arrived as did Margaret at Melrose—where the action was—and Joanne came for two weeks.

We attended a concert a Callymore Hall, and part of the beach crowd planned and participated in the first Sunday picnic bus tour to Barclay Park. The eastern side of the road was set up in banquet style, while across the road, beach people identified their spots to eat, talk, sing, and sleep. The amount and variety of food and drink rivaled Boomers.

As I searched for shells at low tide, someone behind me greeted me asked if I would mind company. I had seen Claude at a distance at Miami Beach. He was always alone on his bicycle. After exchanging names and pleasure for the picnic, we joined the group for pictures and sang our way home to Miami Beach. "See you tomorrow."

Claude Braithwaite was in from the United Kingdom to check on his property that his son and family maintained. I had seen him occasionally on the poolside of the beach. This was supposedly the safer side for children and families, yet this area was the spot where Bertie's first wife drowned, caught in the undertow.

The next week, after his swim, Claude sat at a picnic table near our almond tree hangout and eventually silently joined the group.

As usual, preparation for leaving meant identifying what items Wendy and Clarence would take for storage and what foods Bertie could use, along with my tapes and radio record player.

When I returned several years later to be fully responsible for stocking the fridge and shelves at the apartment at Miami Beach, my concerns were how the fast changes in the island would affect my mobility; how the loss of Eleanora and Dorothy's illness would keep her from coming down, and Mary had only one week in June at her Bouganvillea time share, but Joanne would be down for two weeks. I really had no time to feel lonely if I wanted to.

The Bajan and US partners found me, and our beach group expanded. Bryan was almost as tall as Mike and told "Aunt Florence" all about school, Sunday school, and soccer. I enjoyed a professional visit with Wendy at her day-care program for prekindergarten children with special needs that was housed within a medical facility in Bridgetown. The working parents were difficult to be in contact with. My thought was what about a volunteer vacation? Then I said to myself, *Stop it! Relax, give suggestions, and accept Sunday dinner at her home.*

I continued to relax, read, swim, and hit the slots. These were good memories to have as the year closed with my recuperating from pneumonia. Mary rescued me by a two-week stay at her time-share at the end of May. It took me several months to plan for the next year, but it was worth every minute and dollar spent.

Elaine consented to accompany me for one week to see the island. That allowed me to vacation, relax, and love the land and people. Findlay gave a concert at the St. Gabriel's Church where we met their friends Monica and Horace who drove us home since they lived in Oistins.

At their invitation, we had dinner and long visit with them. Gloria and Deb also landed, and we explored new eateries. Thanks to David, our taxi need to Pottery Village for crafts, lunch, and entertainment provided by a rooster who challenged Elaine all during lunch. At the university, Maurice took Elaine on a tour and shared the plan for expansion. Of course, this was right up Elaine's alley. This visit also ended at lunch. Our beach time, getting to know that family, and time with Wendy exhausted Elaine's seven days. I was overjoyed to have my Bajan friends meet her. She was glad to see the other part of Barbados.

The following weeks were routinely relaxing and I tried not to get caught up in the country's excitement at the unveiling of the statue of Earl Barrow, who had gained their independence from Britain. I questioned why a Chinese company did the work rather than a Bajan construction company. And weren't they still a part of the United Kingdom? What did it mean? To add to my less than exuberance was Dawn's attitude. She was a recent member of the almond tree group who arrived from the UK and was quite open about her disdain of the Bajan gratuitous attitude toward the "snowbirds."

We have since discussed the difference between Beverly's attitude toward her customers and the behavior we witnessed in other settings—supermarkets, hotels, and other places. She subsequently moved from her room near the beach and sought other places to relax. We have kept in touch over the years, and as she was a professional writer; I let her know that if she ever got to New York, Elaine and I would host her while she acquainted with other writers.

My neighbor Burt offered to take me to the nursing home to visit Thelma and pick me up in a couple of hours. I found Thelma in a studio apartment surrounded by her treasures from her four-bedroom house. Having similar experiences, we complained, and then gave thanks for being together, as the Link assembly the previous year, we got a message after three hours that someone was waiting for me.

More adventure awaited, as Burt asked if I minded making a few stops with him throughout the parish of St. John, where acres of prior sugar plantations were now poultry and vegetable farms owned by black Bajan families. A number living elsewhere were successful in sports or business.

The first home we visited was a friend of Burt's who baked pies, which she sold to supermarkets, restaurants, and at the Friday night Oistin's fish fry. Leaving there with a loaf of bread and sweet potato tarts, our next stop was to deliver pastries to a mutual friend of Burt's and his family. I pleaded to stay in the car, although anxious to meet his kin. I was exhausted and bursting from dessert sampling. No slots for me that night—I was just glad to get home and extend my regrets to Beverly by phone.

Joanne came down in time for the picnic. This year, in addition to the old bus, a newer, safer vehicle for seniors was added. We seniors objected to being separated from the group and boarded the old familiar, windowless, hard bench seating bus, and enjoyed the day as usual. Claude made the trip even more enjoyable, as he also deplored the order to separate the group. The last several weeks of that year will stay with me as the exemplification of family reunions.

CHAPTER 11

MIAMI BEACH:
THE ALMOND TREE GANG

O fficially named Enterprise Beach, this strip of manmade beach on the southern coast of Barbados was called "Miami Beach" by the Bajan people. This post popular site on the coast was Beverly's choice to set up her chair-rental business. Separating the beach from the upper road were many other pine and palm trees overlooking the parking spaces, picnic tables, and two-foot-high sea-grape bushes. Centered close to the beach was a magnificent almond tree with branches that spread ten feet across and fan-sized leaves, which provided much-needed shade from the merciless sun and also shelter from the sudden pelting downpour of rain that was common on the island.

It was around and under this tree that the returning nationals and visitors from all parts of the world, but primarily the United Kingdom, United States, and Canada gathered to share the hotels of Patterson, Gresham, and Balducci. We shared the daily newspaper, crossword puzzles, news, weather from home, and any new dinner or jazz spot. Of great concern was each one's living arrangement—location cost, and size—all open to comment and comparison.

Beverly was the center of the beach action. She was five nine, and a young, congenial, sharp businesswoman who worked at the airport's duty-free office since finishing community college. After five years, the government downsized various agencies, and she fell victim. Being thrifty, neither she nor her significant other, Mike, were overly concerned. However, after several attempts at sales, in-terior decorating, and culinary-arts courses, they decided to start a family while awaiting a grand job opportunity. As I had met and made friends with the couple many years before, it seemed important and natural that we "powwow" over this issue with other Albany friends who joined us for a few weeks.

Our thinking was that she should become an entrepreneur. She could sell books; go into business as an interior decorator; make donuts, pizza, or roti. Finally, we suggested renting chairs on the beach. She and Mike felt this was the most doable. With startup support in 1998, she tacked her sign on the almond tree and set up five lounge chairs, boogie boards, and umbrellas. She was busy keeping an eye on her chairs up and the down the beach while interpreting the rental prices in terms of Bajan dollars versus US and Canadian dollars and Euros. She originally stored and set up her inventory single-handed, carrying the chairs across the picnic area and parking lot, up onto the road, and into a rented garage owned by an elderly woman who ran a questionable guest house across the road from the beach. As her business grew, Beverly was able to employ Randall to at least accompany her, and then gradually take full responsibility of setting up by nine thirty and returning everything to storage between five and six.

Randall was called "Fat Man" before losing some pounds. He attempted to clean up. He was the slow but sure, loyal, multitalented guy who, most recently, burst into song and serenaded any listening female. Between set up and storage, he also ran errands for select persons, like the owners of the "Delish" fast-food van and any of the Almond tree gang.

The Almond Tree Gang Picnic

Vivian lived on the island and took on many roles at the beach—the most important being the communication channel between the beach sunbathers and the beach tree shade finders. She had left her grown, married children back in the United Kingdom with maternal and paternal grandparents while she and her husband freed themselves and fled to the warmth and sun of Barbados. What a cook! Her quiche was to-die-for, taken with my variety of local beer and, naturally, rum. Produce from her garden was generously distributed to the gang in exchange for recipes and new ideas for quiche.

Margo was the shining star of the group. Elegant in her nineties, she matched her numerous bikinis and wraps (usually discarded) with earrings, necklaces, ankle bracelets, and shades. She wore a different outfit every day and perfect eye-defining makeup. She provided the spirited conversation as various males, young and old, dropped by to greet the gang and check out any new and interesting persons in the group. She returned home periodically to check in for medical follow-up and visit the family of grandnieces and grandnephews, as well as friends. She drove herself around the island and, most recently, was accompanied by Vivian, who, with the urging and concern of the group, chose to get a lift to and from the beach.

Faye was also an all-day beacher and a nonocean dipper. She read, and aced other crossword puzzles. However, her greatest joy was catering to Bryan, Beverly's son. As he progressed from day care to fourth grade, she became a part of their family, transporting him from school to beach to the Mr. Jingle ice-cream truck playing "Home on the Range" to the "Delish" van. Faye and Vivian covered the business when Beverly attended school meetings or doctor appointments with Bryan.

Faye retired to Barbados from the United Kingdom as a professional emergency-care nurse. After two three-year stints in the Congo and South Africa, she and others became disillusioned about the lack of government concern for the health needs of the people. She revealed her experiences to me, as we discussed a recent best-selling story of missionary work.

Angela was the latest member, but she was a natural. She set up a small beachwear and trinket business. A tall, dark-skinned native Bajan who was fast talking and had a beautiful smile, she was always accommodating. She and her husband eventually closed their neighborhood grocery store as the beachwear business expanded.

Her husband, John, erected a nine-by-nine permanent tent frame to display her merchandise, hats, bags, shoes, and beachwear. He took up full-time photography while transporting Angela from suppliers to the beaches to school for their teenage, college-bound daughter, as well as emergency hospital visits with Angela's mother.

After our first dip in the sea at one o' clock, Eleanora and I joined the group to catch up on the day's gossip. As the two snowbirds in the group, we were always treated royally. Eleanora, through born in Brooklyn, was of Bajan ancestry. We were both in our midseventies when we met at Bernita Apartments in 1995. She had come for three weeks to recuperate from her second colostomy. During that time, we shared news of the sudden death of a relative back home. We supported each other through this and, with other apartment occupants, vowed to keep in touch upon returning to the United States, which we did. During the summer of '95, my usual August gathering brought Eleanor—a new and lively Eleanora—ready to plan for Barbados in '96 but tentatively checking out the possibility of senior housing in Albany, closer to her newfound friends.

In January, I found my usual apartment less than desirable, as the owner was away and had cut the house helpers' hours. I immediately moved to another familiar housekeeping apartment near Dover Beach and called Eleanora to let her know. She recommended Miami Beach Apartments, where she had lived for seven years following her retirement from New York City Transit Authority. This referral worked out well these eleven years.

We both loved the ocean—swimming, exercising, and floating on top the waves—as we identified the various airlines bringing more snowbirds to the beach. She also liked jazz and the slot machines that were just beginning to spread to this part of the island. We discovered that we had shared the same family doctor on Long Island. There were jazz musicians known to us both, as her husband and she had toured with named band leaders until their family, one boy and two girls, arrived. She encouraged him to accept a permanent spot with the NBC orchestra until his death.

As we snowbirds settled in, the group became lively. Hamilton, owner of the home up the beach road, was a favorite visitor who exchanged several barbs with Margo.

While being spoofed by the rest of the group, Cap, also a tall native Bajan, took time between his shoreline cruises business customers to visit and make plans for fun evenings with any and all takers.

Carlos, Michael, and Bratha were also friends of the gang. However, Adrian was awaited anxiously each day. A partially blind, five-foot-ten Rasta man who traveled by a bicycle that had been fitted to hold a cooler for fruits ranging from apples, pears, grapes, and tangerines and a ten-gallon plastic sack containing a one-dollar packets of roasted peanuts and candies.

He usually arrived between two thirty and three, parked his bike near the tree, and serviced the needs of the gang first. Then he found his way down "Miami Beach." There was no bargaining; grapes were one dollar. Apples, pears, and tangerines were either two for one dollar or one dollar each, depending on the season and availability.

In February '03, Angela suggested a Sunday picnic for the gang—family and friends—including food and a tour. Cap entertained with his guitar, accompanied by Angela's superb contralto voice, while others napped under the east-coast trees of Barclay Park, and some searched for shells along the rough shore. The trip in the retired open-air yellow bus was a marvel to the residents as the loud singing, cheering, waving group made their way home after consuming fifty pounds of chicken, yams, potato salad, tossed salad, cake, ham, fish, and cases of beer laced with individual choices of rum and vodka.

By 2004, the tourism authority designated Beverly and Angela's spot as an official vendors' area. We were thrilled upon visiting the site. However, by 2007, I was stunned to see just the stripped ten-foot trunk of the almond tree. The original sign was still there, tacked and wired. The tree had been declared dead by the beach authorities, and they stripped branches and bark, leaving a naked reminder of the majestic almond tree. Did it just die of disease as had Eleanora in '04, Faye in '05, and Margo in '06, or was there something else going on? Someone's need to disperse, dissolve, and destroy the group. Vivian no longer attended the beach. Working and visiting the family in England takes her time.

Brewster came around at four thirty to spar with Randall and work on su-
doku puzzles. The picnic this year was different, and it was too far for me, as
there were two buses, a yellow one and a newer transport bus on which the "elders" were encouraged to board along with the youngsters. We firmly declined.
We enjoyed the freedom and discomfort of old yellow. Myra and Dawn joined
the group to support the ongoing infusion of Almond Tree folk both were six- to
nine-month month visitors. Myra was from the United States; Dawn was from
the United Kingdom.

I shall visit for short stays, but I miss the Almond Tree Gang.

F. Frazier March, 2007

Pleasure is the flower that fades;
Remembrance is the
Lasting perfume.
—Stanislas Boufflers

REFLECTIONS

I owe my life of freedom and joy to Mom, who allowed me to explore and get to know people and then supplemented my knowledge of our own diverse, multifaith neighborhood, community, and all of the United States. She understood this second daughter whose love of school, pleasure of being with people, and independence reflected so much of herself. From parent and child to partners in raising a family to adult seniors alone, the bond was never broken, even as my peer friends, work associates, partners along the way left or took other pathways, and new journeymen were opening doors of friendship and adventure that I explored. I gained happiness and joy from an ever-committed busy, traveled world to which I give thanks.

DEDICATION

To all the younger family members who are questioning their future, believe and keep the faith. All people are on the same road to somewhere. We all make our own choices and deal with the consequences.

To my nephews and nieces, grand and great, and to my precious Kiara, who is so much of my unfinished story. You must know that we stand on great shoulders, the Civil War widow with three children to raise who is fighting for a pension that she finally received twenty-six years later. Her daughter, Ruth, and her mate, George Johnson, worked on the estate of an English couple, the Youngs. And Ruth and George's daughter, Clara, my mom—a strong and undaunted woman.

Act of June 27, 1890.

N° 463189

Original.

UNITED STATES of AMERICA

DEPARTMENT of the INTERIOR

BUREAU OF PENSIONS

It is hereby certified That in conformity with the laws of the United States _Eleanor J. Smith_ Widow of _Moses Smith_ who was a Private, Co. E, 26 Regt. United States Colored Vol. Inf. is entitled to a pension at the rate of _Eight_ dollars per month, to commence on the _Fifteenth_ day of _August_ 1891 and to continue during her widowhood.

Given at the Department of the Interior this _Fifth_ day of _July_, one thousand eight hundred and ninety-_Eight_, and of the Independence of the United States of America the one hundred and _Twenty-second_.

Cornelius N. Bliss
Secretary of the Interior.

Countersigned:
H. Clay Evans
Commissioner of Pensions.

Bereau of Pensions (F)

That section forty-seven hundred and sixty-five, title fifty-seven of the Revised Statutes of the United States is hereby amended to read as follows:

Sec. 4745.—Any pledge, mortgage, sale, assignment, or transfer of any right, claim, or interest in any pension which has been, or may hereafter be, granted, shall be void and of no effect; and any person who shall pledge, or receive as a pledge, mortgage, sale, assignment or transfer of any right, claim, or interest in any pension, or pension certificate, which has been, or may hereafter be, granted or issued, or who shall hold the same as collateral security for any debt, or promise, or upon any pretext of such security, or promise, shall be guilty of a misdemeanor; and upon conviction thereof shall be fined in a sum not exceeding one hundred dollars and the costs of the prosecution; and any person who shall retain the certificate of a pensioner and refuse to surrender the same upon the demand of the Commissioner of Pensions, or a United States pension agent, or any other person, authorized by the Commissioner of Pensions, or the pensioner, to receive the same shall be guilty of a misdemeanor; and upon conviction thereof shall be fined in a sum not exceeding one hundred dollars and the costs of the prosecution.

Approved February 28, 1883.

Bereau of Pensions (B)

Honorable Discharge from The United States Army

FEB 24 1919

Paid in full... 170.6
Camp Upton, L. I.
J. E. Adams
1st Lt. Q.M.C.U.S.A.

TO ALL WHOM IT MAY CONCERN:

This is to Certify, That* James H. Jackson
1103954, Private, Co G 369th Infantry

THE UNITED STATES ARMY, *as a* TESTIMONIAL OF HONEST AND FAITHFUL

SERVICE, *is hereby* HONORABLY DISCHARGED *from the military service of the*

UNITED STATES *by reason of* ‡

Said James H. Jackson _____ *was born*

in Huntington, L. I., *in the State of* New York

When enlisted he was 19 *years of age and by occupation a* Laborer

He had Brown *eyes,* Black *hair,* Colored *complexion, and*

was 5 *feet* 9 *inches in height.*

Given under my hand at Camp Upton N.Y. *this*

24th *day of* February *one thousand nine hundred and* nineteen

Colonel
Commanding.

O. G. APR 29 1919
C. E. GRAY,
Maj. O.M. Corps.

Form No. 525, A. G. O.
Oct. 9-18.

*Insert name, Christian name first: e. g., "John Doe."
†Insert Army serial number, grade, company and regiment or arm or corps or department; a. g., "1,620,810"; "Corporal, Company A, 1st Infantry"; "Sergeant, Quartermaster Corps"; "Sergeant, First Class, Medical Department."
‡If discharged prior to expiration of service, give number, date, and source of order or full description of authority therefor.

James Jackson Army Discharge (F)

ENLISTMENT RECORD.

Name: *James H. Jackson* Grade: *Private*

Enlisted or inducted, *June 10*, 191*7*, at *Huntington L.I., NY*

Serving in *First* enlistment period at date of discharge.

Prior service: * *None*

Noncommissioned officer: *None*

Marksmanship, gunner qualification or rating: ? *Not Rated*

Horsemanship: *Not Mounted*

Battles, engagements, skirmishes, expeditions: *Champagne, Argonne Forests, Alsace*

Knowledge of any vocation: *Laborer*

Wounds received in service: *None*

Physical condition when discharged: *Good*

Typhoid prophylaxis completed *Sept. 17, 1917*

Paratyphoid prophylaxis completed *Sept. 17, 1917*

Married or single: *Single*

Character: *Very Good*

Remarks: *No absences under G.O.*

Signature of soldier: *James Henry Jackson*

Lou J Jadlos
1st Lieut 369 Infantry
Commanding *U.S.*

James Jackson Army Discharge (B)